Paragraph
Structure
Inference

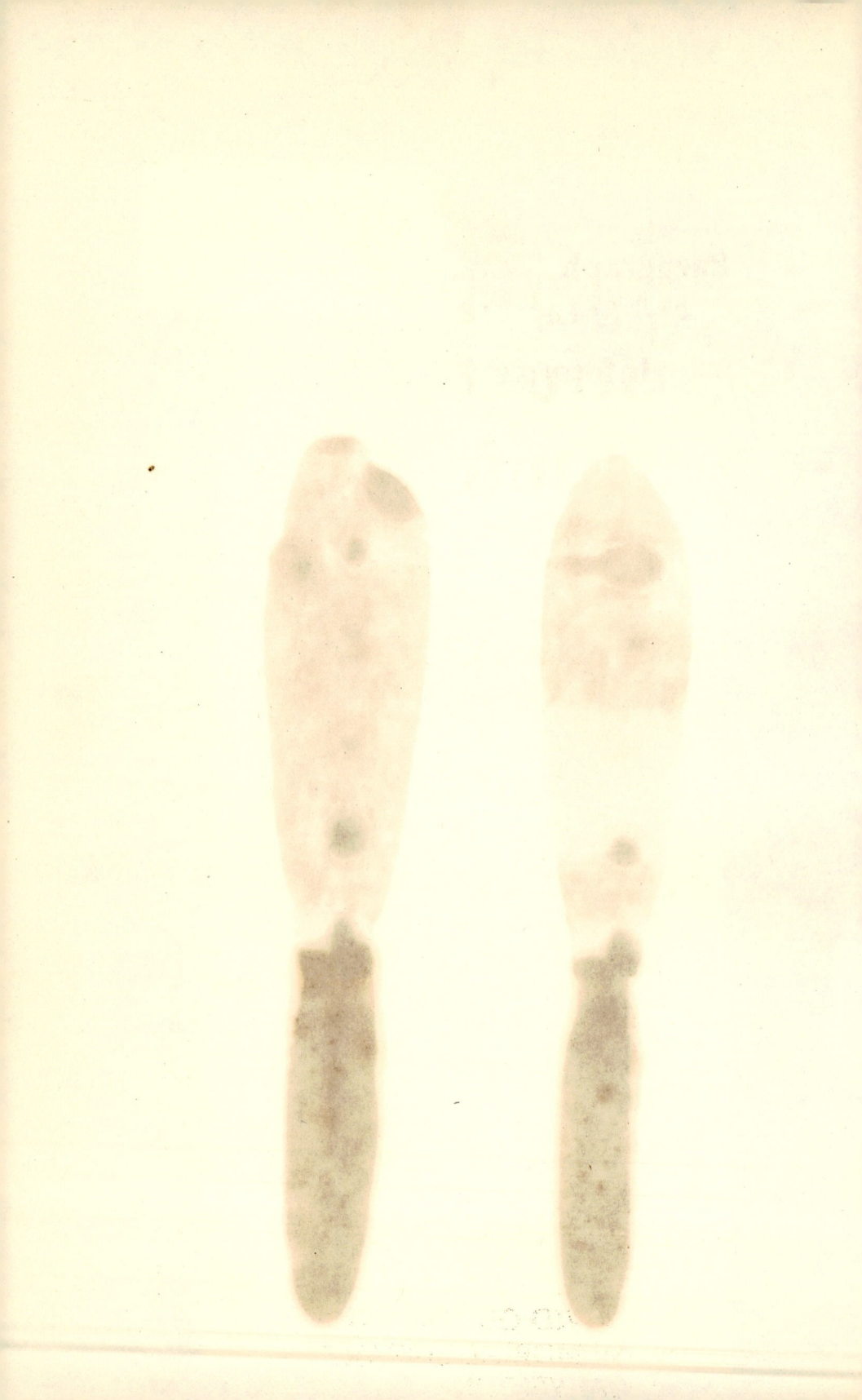

Paragraph Structure Inference

Edward J. Crothers
University of Colorado

Ablex Publishing Corporation
Norwood, New Jersey 07648

Printed in the United States of America

Library of Congress Cataloging in Publication Data

Crothers, Edward J.
   Paragraph structure inference.

   Bibliography: p.
   Includes index.
   1. Paragraphs.   2. Inference (Logic)   I. Title.
P302.C7   415   78-27307
ISBN   0-89391-016-3

ABLEX Publishing Corporation
355 Chestnut Street
Norwood, New Jersey 07648

Contents

Tables

Preface

A foremost current problem within linguistics, psychology and education is the development of a theory of text structure. Within linguistics, the text level of analysis is now being recognized as no less fundamental to language description than is the much better understood sentence level. Within psychology, a theory capable of yielding a comprehensive analysis of a paragraph or a longer text through the application of explicit general principles would significantly benefit the active research programs currently under way in psychological and artificial intelligence studies of reading comprehension. Such a theory might also be of practical value to the concerns of educational psychology. An adequate method of representing a text's structure is prerequisite in devising procedures for improving a reader's understanding and memory of that text.

A theory responsive to these multidisciplinary needs must satisfy certain requirements. It must yield comprehensive structure descriptions derived from general principles. The principles, it will be argued, must be formulated at the text level of analysis and include rules of inference based on the notion of text *coherence* (or *cohesion*). Currently, no theory meets these conditions. However, progress in this direction can be seen in a number of approaches, beginning with the early linguistic work of Harris (1952) and continuing to the more recent linguistic and cognitive developments (Crothers, 1972; van Dijk, 1973; Frederiksen, 1975b; Gopnik, 1972; Grimes, 1975; Halliday & Hasan, 1976; Kintsch, 1974; Rumelhart, 1975; Schank, 1975b).

Paragraph Structure Inference presents an inference-based theory of text structure intended to meet these requirements and to lend itself to these applications. The theory is intended primarily for written texts, since it contains no prosodic component to describe a text's phonological properties. This book is organized into eight chapters. The first chapter states the book's objectives, basic issues, and relationships to other research. The second chapter sets forth the general theory together with a statistical comparison of the outcomes of applications to brief passages. The third chapter gives some useful additional theoretical analyses. Each of the next four chapters is a detailed application to a particular brief passage. The final chapter is an extension to a somewhat longer and more complex text, examining only its inferential structure. In terms of inferences, the order of these five applications is from the simplest text to the most complex.

The main contributions of this book are the following:

The rationale for the theory, based on what are taken to be the basic issues facing any text theory, is treated in Chapter 1.2.

For deriving the underlying text structure from the explicit surface text, the fundamental developments are the formulation of proposition and element inferences in Chapter 2.3.1 and connective inferences in Chapter 3.3.

For describing the explicit text itself, the key notions appear in Chapter 2.3.2.

Supplementary analyses of information newness and of text summarization are found in Chapters 3.2 and 3.4, respectively.

A comparison of four text structures, in terms of their relative frequencies of different characteristics, accompanies the introduction to the general theory in Chapter 2 and likewise the supplementary analyses in Chapter 3.

As to applications to individual brief passages, the layout of the representations and their derivations is introduced in Chapter 4 for a passage whose structure is relatively simple.

Next come Chapters 5-7, which demonstrate the analysis of successively more complex passages. Here the general formulation of inferences is brought to bear on inferentially more interesting texts. Each of these sections ends with a summary subsection giving an informal profile of the structure description as revealed by the analysis.

Finally, Chapter 8 is the one extension to a lengthier text. More to the point, the application is to a text whose inferential structure is exceptionally interesting. Comparisons with previous formulations by other theorists, including a story grammar alternative, are discussed.

The theory presented here was developed over a period of about eight years. An earlier version appeared in a 1972 volume, *Language Comprehension and the Acquisition of Knowledge,* edited by John B. Carroll and Roy Freedle. That volume is a report of a 1971 workshop funded and administered by the Committee on Basic Research in Education (COBRE), formerly a committee within the U.S. Office of Education. However, the early versions of the theory are rather more primitive and superficial than the much more advanced formulation presented here. The influence of the early formulations is no longer directly recognizable in the present version, so in fact this book could more accurately be described as a new theory rather than a new version of a former theory. The early formulation addressed chiefly the representation of an explicit text, and lacked the cohesion-based theory of text inference that undergirds the present approach.

The first draft of the cohesion-based analysis appeared in a 1975 technical report (Crothers, 1975). Further significant progress in both the theory and the exposition have culminated in the present work. As to exposition, the originally oversized tables have been organized more compactly, and the accompanying discussions have been abridged by deleting certain details and secondary analyses. As to substance, the classification of inferences and its associated terminology have been modified. Both the treatment of connectives and that of information newness have been reformulated. A final chapter has been added extending the theory to another passage, *Circle Island*. The attractions of that passage are that it is longer than the others analyzed here, it is rich in inferences, and it has previously been analyzed from several other approaches. In sum, the aim of this book is to present more a conceptual framework and less a manual of analysis procedures than was done in 1975 technical report. A brief summary of the inference component of the theory was published recently (Crothers, 1978a), and another paper (Crothers, 1978b) included an earlier version of the Chapter 8 analysis.

Except for the last chapter this work was supported by a National Science Foundation Grant, GB-34077X, administered by the Institute for the Study of Intellectual Behavior, the Graduate School, the University of Colorado at Boulder. Support for the final chapter was provided by the National Institute of Education, Grant G-77-0011.

Edward J. Crothers

Paragraph
Structure
Inference

1. The Objectives

1.1 INTRODUCTION

This book presents a linguistic-logical theory of paragraph and text descriptive representation. The theory is intended to be both a linguistic theory and a basis for psychological and educational applications to research on reading comprehension and memory. Such applications are left for the future, however. The first chapters develop the general principles, which are then invoked in the later chapters to derive or discuss the representations of five brief text passages. The analysis itself is at the text level rather than either the sentence level or the knowledge level. Fundamental to this theory is the notion of text *coherence* or *cohesion.* This notion underlies the formulation of principles of text inference, which is the primary component of the theory although it has been insufficiently appreciated in current linguistic approaches. Accompanying the treatment of inferences is a description of the explicit text itself, including a text information classification and procedures for generating summaries. For extension to longer texts, methods of simplifying the descriptions are suggested. In relation to psychological and educational research, the theory is neither a process model nor a method for editing a text. Instead, it is a foundation for research on both of these significant current problems.

The objective of this book is to develop a theory that is at once general in its range of applicability and specific in its text level descriptions. The proposed theoretical principles are indeed general despite their having been formulated in the immediate context of only five brief text passages, because in fact they derive from language structure itself. Notably, the treatment of inferences amounts to an extension of the notions of presupposition, premise, and consequence. Also, to counterbalance the fact that only five passages are analyzed, the five were selected from two different rhetorical modes, argumentative and narrative, as well as from diverse styles with respect to attributes such as explicitness-implicitness and pointedness-diffuseness. The resulting ensemble of propositions, a few hundred in number by one way of counting, does indeed suggest principles applicable to texts in general.

The structure description produced for an individual passage is more complete and specific—at the text level of analysis—than that achieved by any other approach to date. Furthermore, the rationale for each specific feature of the description is set forth as explicitly as possible in any system that must in part deal with admittedly subjective inferences. Each of the first four chapters on an application, after first presenting a passage's derived underlying structure, is devoted to the derivation of that structure. Every inference or other aspect of the derivation is justified by citing the general rule applied. In this way the analysis avoids a major problem in current propositional theories (Anderson, 1976, p. 29): "This failure to specify a procedure for assigning representations to sentences is common to all current propositional theories and has serious consequences for all of the theories."

Unavoidably and unsurprisingly, the depth of the resulting descriptions combined with the rigorous derivation of those descriptions produces an analysis that is extremely detailed when presented in full. On first thought the theory might therefore be judged too detailed to be feasible for most text research purposes. Consequently it is necessary to dispel any such impression. In fact, the theory can be adapted to yield a greater or lesser depth of analysis depending on the requirements of any particular experimental, theoretical, or educational objective. It can be argued that useful simplifying approximations to a text's full description come about more insightfully as a direct consequence of a prior development of general principles than as a superficial alternative to such principles. In short, we can expect the natural evolution of the theory to begin with the initial detailed analysis of brief text passages, intended to establish the soundness of the principles, and continue to the later more overall analysis of longer texts, intended to establish the applicability of the principles. Most of the present volume is restricted to the initial formulation, but simplifications suggest themselves rather directly, as will be seen especially in Chapter 8.

To cope with the depth of detail, the exposition has been systematically arranged, especially in Chapters 4-7. Each entire derived text structure, and likewise each derivation itself, has been compactly represented in tables and figures, leaving the remainder of the chapter to serve only as accompanying commentary. Each commentary is organized so that all occurrences of the same derivational principle are discussed together, enabling the reader to skip those of lesser interest to him. Finally, each application section ends with an informal summary of the passage's profile based on all analyses.

Before turning to the basic issues that influenced the formulation of the theory, it would be helpful to give a concrete example of the sort of description it yields. Consider the following two paragraphs, which are among the brief text passages to be analyzed in detail. A title has been added to each passage for convenience in referring to it. The first is an excerpt from a famous political essay by Thoreau (1849):

THE STATE

> I saw that the state was half-witted, that it was timid as a lone woman with her silver spoons, and that it did not know its friends from its foes, and I lost all my remaining respect for it, and pitied it. Thus, the state never intentionally confronts a man's sense, intellectual or moral, but only his body, his senses. It is not armed with superior wit or honesty, but with superior physical strength. I was not born to be forced. I will breathe after my own fashion.

The second is a narrative paragraph presented in, and evidently originally composed for, some psychological experiments on memory (Pompi & Lachman, 1967; Yuille & Paivio, 1969.)

THE OPERATION

> Chief Resident Jones adjusted his face mask while anxiously surveying a pale figure secured to the long gleaming table before him. One swift stroke of his small sharp instrument and a thin red line appeared. Then an eager young assistant carefully extended the opening as another aide pushed aside glistening surface fat so that vital parts were laid bare. Everyone present stared in horror at ugly growth too large for removal. He now knew it was pointless to continue.

The passages differ in their semantic content, of course, but that is the domain of a semantic level theory. They also differ remarkably in their text level structure, the very thing that a theory of text structure must represent. The differences range from the more immediately obvious and easy to formulate to the deeper and conceptually more interesting. In fact, upon analysis it turns out that in a very fundamental respect, namely inferences, these two paragraphs are at the opposite extremes of the five brief passages to be analyzed in this volume—which is why they have been selected here to exemplify the comparisons. The following informal synopsis of both passages' analyses will suggest the depth of description possible for a single passage and consequently the wealth of comparisons possible between passages.

Upon analysis, *State* is found to be a structurally simple, tightly written argumentative paragraph embodying metaphor and contrast. The passage is predominantly abstract rather than concrete (though this property is really lexical, not textual). Figurative speech, especially anthropomorphic metaphor, is employed in order to dramatize the abstract argument. The coherence of the paragraph—an intuitively familiar notion which will be refined into a key concept of the present theory—suffers from an ambiguity, which like the other properties is precisely describable. A major feature of the paragraph is that it includes no inferences of entire propositions. Another important property is that inferences of propositional elements, not entire propositions, are quite routine though only moderately frequent. The paragraph is relatively tightly written from the standpoint of its skillful exploitation of certain lexical relations. To provide some relief from the rigid structure, several forms of stylistic variation are used. Another analysis reveals the passage to be comparatively high in both old information and in what will be called contrastive information. Also, the classification of the logical-semantic propositional connectives shows that in *State* the most prevalent connectives are those either for semantic consequence or for identity. Finally, another analysis demonstrates that the paragraph has a succinct summary.

Structurally, *Operation* is very different from *State*. Now one encounters many nontrivial inferences of entire propositions, in fact more propositions implicit than explicit. The inference types are also quite varied, exemplifying in one paragraph many of the most important types recognized for texts in general. Without yet going into detail, one of the major inferences is of the consequent theme of the entire passage, while another is of a step mediating between two explicit propositions. Element inferences are also numerous, diverse, and often nontrivial. The differences from *State* are hardly limited to the inferential aspect, however. There are few notable lexical relations in *Operation*. This, coupled with the relative lack of old or contrastive information, contributes to a sense of loose organization. The coherence, however, is unambiguous. Being a narrative, the passage might be expected to have as its principal connectives those that express temporal succession. But when the connectives to and among inferred propositions are included, semantic consequence is found here also to be a prominent role of the connectives. The passage cannot be concisely summarized, unless simply by its inferred consequent.

These two examples impart a glimpse of what is probably the most surprising outcome of the five applications, namely the manifold diversity of text structures. The theory of text structure presented here allows an in-depth description of this diversity. Of course, applying only part of the theory would yield simpler approximate descriptions and comparisons. In keeping with the theoretical nature of this book, however, no speculations will be offered at this time on the possible psychological or educational implications of these two particular descriptions, though some conjectures will be ventured later, in the course of actually developing the analyses.

1.2 BASIC ISSUES

The formulation of this theory was guided by several specific and basic considerations. They are as follows:

1.   Since the purpose of this work was to develop a theory applicable to psycholinguistic research, it was deemed more directly appropriate to formulate

principles for the descriptive analysis of given passages than to undertake a formal generative grammar that would characterize only the more abstract properties of texts in general (van Dijk, 1973; Petöfi, 1973). There would appear to be no reason why a corresponding text grammar could not be developed, however. For example, a modest beginning might include a few simple rules, such as $\P \to C + A$, $C \to C + A$, $C \to C + C$, $A \to C + A$, and $A \to A + A$, where the symbols $\P$, A, and C denote, respectively, a paragraph, an antecedent proposition, and a consequent proposition, and "+" denotes a connective. (Obviously, many more rules would need to be added.) A paragraph analysis given by the present theory does yield a tree graph equivalent of certain generative rules, but of course only those pertaining to that particular paragraph, not for texts in general. A generative text grammar would be valuable, for instance in comparing paragraphs or ascertaining their complexity. But it would seem to encounter at least one significant problem—the world knowledge limitation. At the level of a sentence grammar one knows enough about many lexical concepts to be able to compose innumerable semantically acceptable sentences containing them. For example, for a very large number of noun phrases in the lexicon, an adult's vocabulary knowledge would be sufficient to supply a verb phrase that would complete a semantically acceptable sentence. On the other hand, given an entire sentence it would seem less likely that with equal facility the sane adult could generate, say, a nontrivial coherent consequent of it. In graph terms, the terminal nodes would ordinarily be more difficult to fill in for a text grammar than for a sentence grammar. This conjecture appears consistent with the notion of codability in a language. A concept expressed by a proposition (or, more precisely, the nominalization of that proposition) is ordinarily less codable, less familiar, than one which has occurred so frequently that it has already been abbreviated to a word of its own.

The fact that the present theory does not generate texts does not mean that it has no role to play in text composition, however. One need not stop with the analysis of a given passage; one can then edit it in the light of the structure revealed by the analysis. Frequently an analysis will suggest a few opportunities for editing a passage by nontrivial, nonobvious explication and reorganization rather than merely by obvious mechanical correction. Of course, the benefit from such editing can only be assessed experimentally, but at least the theory suggests the editing in the first place. In this volume no attempt has been made to formulate the principles of editing, however. Additionally, one can certainly see that it might be wise to edit some texts as a simplifying preliminary to the analysis, but such intuitive preediting tends to be more piecemeal and fortuitous than theoretically motivated postediting.

Another related basic question is this: If the rules of the theory are not to be organized into a grammar, how then are they to be organized? It has seemed best to collect them in a taxonomy, one taxonomy for each general class of rules. Hence, a classification of proposition inferences will be proposed, another for connective inferences, and several others as well. At once there arises the question of which is more felicitous—a fairly simple and broad classification or a more elaborately refined one. The position adopted here, somewhat reluctantly, is that in practice a moderately elaborate classification is actually better, despite its initial apparent complexity. The reason is that the motivation for refining a classification, in this volume at any rate, is not so much the comprehensiveness of the taxonomy as the ease of application to actual passenges. One does not have to analyze many passages in order to appreciate the great variety of surface forms encountered. The more subtypes included in the classification, the easier it is to find one similar enough to a new one to facilitate its analysis.

2. A fundamental characteristic of this text structure theory is that it takes the level of analysis to be the text itself. A text theory should yield the structure of a text *qua* text, as distinct from its syntactic and semantic structures; the level of analysis should be the text, not the sentence or word. Reasonably adequate theories of sentence syntax and sentence and word semantics are well known. Merely taking such a theory and applying it to an entire text sentence-by-sentence does not produce a text structure, but only a text's syntactic structure. It is important to add, however, that this does not mean that semantic information can be disregarded in the analysis. On the contrary, knowledge of meanings and factual information is essential in order to derive the text inferences. Word meanings and the like are therefore used in deriving the representation but are not themselves represented. To do so would require a full semantic theory, probably either in the form of an analysis into a network of nonprimitive concepts (Quillian, 1969; Rumelhart, Lindsay, & Norman, 1972) or in the form of configurations of semantic primitives (Schank, 1975a).

The insistence on text structure as a level of analysis in its own right has major practical consequences for the description of a given text. Because no claim is being made that syntactic and semantic descriptions are being provided, those components can be left to current syntactic-semantic theories. Such a division of labor is not only justifiable, it is practically essential if the text component is to be derived without becoming obscured by the syntactic and semantic details. Such details could easily become overwhelming if pursued at length. To cite a couple of extreme examples of detailed syntactic and semantic analyses, Ross (1974, p. 129) finds no fewer than 22 propositions underlying the sentence *Floyd broke the glass,* while Katz (1972, p. 165) derives a very complex lexical representation for the verb *chase.* Obviously, a text level theory cannot become enmeshed in such microanalyses for every sentence and word in the text. Concerning syntax, the present approach assumes a syntactic analysis of sentences into what are called propositions. The assumed analysis would, of course, employ accepted principles for decomposition, recovery of syntactic deletions, and so on. But the details of the syntactic aspect of the derivation of propositions from sentences will be left unstated here. In most cases the derivations, at least to a degree of syntactic detail sufficient for text description, are routine. Moreover, some of the pertinent syntactic details have been discussed previously (Crothers, 1975). Besides omitting the justification of the syntactic analyses, the other simplification is that certain syntactic constructions have been left syntactically complex instead of being fully broken down into their ultimate constitutents. Certain analyzable phrases have been left unanalyzed. Certain complex surface clauses have been left as such instead of being broken down into syntactically elementary clauses.

Likewise, no semantic component, either for sentential semantics (e.g., tautology, analyticity, as in Katz, 1972) or for lexical semantics (e.g., semantic primitives, as in Schank, 1975a) accompanies the present text level description. The question of whether lexical decomposition of words does or does not occur in comprehension is really a question about processing. To be consistent, a coherence-based text theory must claim that lexical information is textually relevant only if it contributes to the coherence of the text. For example, if a text sentence contained the phrases *a chimpanzee,* then neither the feature *+ primate* (nor any other feature, for that matter) is inherently text level information; it belongs to lexical semantics. But suppose the text later contained the phrase *this primate.* Then the description would indeed connect the former phrase to the latter, because the connection augments the text coherence. As a second example, in some passages the semantic feature *+ animate* recurs so often that it can be used as the label for one of the main categories of that text. Its textual significance derives only from the frequent recurrence in that particular text.

For a text level theory, then, what notion might occupy a position of central importance, comparable to the notion of grammaticality at the sentence level? As stated earlier, the basic text notion is *coherence* or *cohesion.* A main purpose of many, though not all, of the proposed inference types is to explicate the implicit coherence of the passage. Inferences of connectivity serve to identify unstated relations to presupposition, antecedence, consequence, and so forth, that hold among propositions. Many of the proposition inferences produce intermediate steps between explicit antecedent and explicit consequent, thus strengthening the cohesion between the two. An inferred consequent or antecedent of two or more propositions enhances the cohesion between them by showing that together they function as an antecedent or consequent, respectively. Inferences of referential antecedents link propositions together through the relationships of coreference. Lexical relationships such as synonymy or antonymy also contribute to the coherence. In all, coherence thus includes connectivity, coreferentiality, and lexical comparison or contrast.

The concept of coherence offers something essential to text analysis, namely a criterion for deciding which of the many possible inferences from the explicit text are worth including in the representation (cf. Schank, 1975b). The more a given inferable proposition contributes to coherence, the more one should be inclined to include it. This means that the same inferable proposition could be included in one text's representation but excluded from another's. For example, if in one text the inferable proposition was only weakly linked to the text, say by being an antecedent or consequent of only one text proposition, it could then be excluded. But in another text the very same inferable proposition might be the overall consequent theme, with the coherence of the explicit text accruing from its role as antecedent for that consequent. In this case the inferable proposition should certainly be represented. Note that this criterion for propositions is consistent with the criterion for propositional elements mentioned earlier using the *chimpanzee* example.

Given a coherent text, the next key concept is that of a text's *theme;* which term will be used here to mean the propositions most central to the text's development. It will be maintained that in a connection between an antecedent proposition or propositions and a consequent, the consequent is always thematic in relation to the antecedent. There is no need to restrict this principle to those cases in which the consequent is explicit, for following Grimes (1975, Chap. 21), one can distinguish the theme from its surface manifestation, if any, the *topic.* As will be illustrated later, this principle obviates any set of numerous highly specialized subrules (Rumelhart, 1975). Several observations support the proposal. First, the overall consequent is usually found near the beginning or the end of the passage, precisely where it would be expected if it was indeed the theme. Also, when a passage does explicitly state its main theme, the conclusion is usually what is identified. Finally, a major consequent usually contains fewer propositions than its antecedents collectively do, which would be expected if the two correspond to theme and development of theme, respectively. This principle hardly originates with the present theory, of course. It goes back at least to William James, who said ". . . for the important thing about a train of thought is its conclusion." (1891, p. 168).

3. A text level theory, if it is to represent coherence and also be psychologically realistic, must differ fundamentally from a closed logic or syntax. The theory must include plausible inferences that depend on world knowledge, which itself is necessarily outside the theory since no theory can encompass all knowledge. In thus acknowledging the importance of world knowledge for structure analysis, the theory is closer to artificial intelligence models of natural language processing, such as Schank's (1975a) or Winograd's (1972), than to any system that recognizes only those inferences which necessarily follow from its axioms. A most significant property of plausible inferences is that they are judgmental. Two individuals can, and often will, differ in their judgments as to whether or not a proposed inference is at all plausible. This is a familiar phenomenon. For instance, take the following sentence from one of the paragraphs to be analyzed: *It has been suggested that the reason Napoleon lost the Battle of Leipzig was that he ate a peach after the Battle of Dresden.* A plausible inference here, but one that is no more than plausible, is that of proposition *Napoleon became ill* intervening as a possible effect of his eating the peach and in turn a possible cause of his losing the next battle. But certainly different readers could

disagree as to how salient this particular inference is. Being a synthetic inference, it is falsifiable, though not necessarily false, on the basis of world knowledge. (For instance, it is not analytically impossible that Napoleon's eating of the peach might have angered some striking fruit pickers, who rebelled and disrupted his military campaign.) The significant conclusion from this discussion is that the expression "*the* structure of a text" is misleading. It connotes a single, unvarying structure, when in fact all that can exist is a structure relative to one or another body of world knowledge—which knowledge may, but need not, exhibit high agreement between individuals.

An important general consequence here is this: The inherent plausibility rather than certainty of world knowledge inferences should not be allowed to obfuscate the evaluation of a proposed theory of text structure. When the theory is applied to a particular passage, all that can legitimately be demanded is that the application include those inferences which seem plausible by one or another acceptable criterion, such as the theorist's own judgment or a consensus of judgments. Within reasonable limits, it is better to represent too many inferences than too few; some might then be recognized even though they might not be produced spontaneously, and others might be overlooked because they are too commonplace. Above all, none can be judged unless it has been previously formulated. But the theory stands or falls on its general principles. It is not invalidated by a particular questionable inference any more than a grammar is invalidated because its proponent happens to make a dubious judgment as to the grammaticality or ambiguity of some particular sentence.

4. Looking toward future applications of the theory, a foremost issue is the devising of simplifying approximations to substitute for the complete description. Such simplifications would facilitate the application to larger numbers of short texts and, by the same token, to longer texts as well. Though the matter has not been seriously studied yet, this theory does suggest several natural ways to proceed. The description is already an intentional major simplification, of course, since only the text level is represented. Within the text description itself there are several additional directions worth exploring. The common principle behind them is that, given the various derivational operations identified by the theory, systematic approximations can be obtained by foregoing all instances of operations deemed less interesting for a given purpose and performing only the remaining types, thus yielding a partial description. This segregation of derivational operations produces an adaptable architecture for the theory as a whole, resembling the modular approach that has been advocated in artificial intelligence (Winograd, 1972).

Another major simplification would be to take a larger unit of analysis than a single proposition, in order to concentrate on the macrostructure of connections between different paragraphs or sections of a longer text. Other serious possibilities for a longer text would be to limit the within-paragraph representation to the theme of each paragraph, or else to limit the entire text analysis to the more thematic levels of the text as a whole. One other direction for simplification would be to limit the analysis to the inferences, foregoing the within-proposition categorization and other analyses of the explicit text. A quite different strategy would be to exploit a text sampling technique. Every author has his or her own characteristic style; hence from a detailed analysis of short segments of a single text one should be able to estimate descriptive parameters for the text as a whole. Text comparisons also suggest a direction for simplification, namely by focusing on those aspects that create the impression of distinguishing one style from another. Finally, from the psychological standpoint one likely direction for simplifying is to disregard those features expected from past research to be the most routine for comprehension, such as the more commonplace types of referential inferences.

5.   Again looking toward future applications of this theory, there arises the major question of exactly what a text structure theory can contribute to the understanding of text comprehension. Process models of comprehension and memory, though not dealt with as such in this volume, are never very far in the background. By now it is generally recognized that structure and process go hand in hand—how we know depends on what we know. Of course, it also depends on other well-known factors such as task-induced cognitive strategies, short-term memory capacity, and perceptual and motivational conditions. The necessity but not sufficiency of a structure analysis is, of course, true of cognition generally. For text research in particular, the theory, when applied to a passage, identifies the inferences and from them the underlying text structure representing the idealized outcome of comprehension. The more adequately one can represent the structure, the better is his ability to define the transformation between input structure and output structure performed by a process model. Hence, the ability to infer what the process model must have been to produce that transformation is also increased. This holds true regardless of whether one chooses to view structure as directly represented in memory, or as producible one piece at a time from a set of stored processes with associated inputs.

By the same token, the structure theory alone does not require one to adopt one particular experimental psychological hypothesis in preference to any other; this is the very province of a process model. To cite an especially interesting example, the structure theory can identify the inferences in a passage as a prerequisite to experiments on how inferences affect comprehension. But the structure theory neither implies that a terse, inexplicit inversion of a text is more comprehensible than a painstakingly explicit version, nor that it is less comprehensible. In sum, the potential role of the theory in cognitive research is methodological: the analysis of structure to stimulate thinking about process models, the guiding of the construction of experimental passages to test such models, and finally the means of data analysis of subjects' protocols that are themselves paragraphs, in order to evaluate the models.

1.3 RELATED APPROACHES

This brief survey will be restricted to text research in the last few decades. A serious tracing of the historical origins would, of course, have to go back much further—to Aristotle's "enthymemes" (incomplete arguments) in rhetoric, for example. Within modern linguistics the first formal theory of text structure is due to Harris (1952), whose framework has been extended in later studies (Gopnik, 1972). The scope of the theory is much too narrow, evidently because the focus is limited only to discourse classes and other properties that are derivable syntactically. Another early approach exhibits a much broader perspective (Pike, 1954; Longacre, 1972), but an attempt to formalize it (Loriot & Hollenbach, 1970) again narrows the description to only those text properties most readily incorporated.

A very interesting recent linguistic theory of discourse in general is that of Grimes (1975). Grimes proposes a number of principles of text structure, including types of information, partitioning of information, and three levels of organization of information (Halliday, 1967) called *content, cohesion,* and *staging.* In general, each of these concepts has a counterpart in the present system, though the relationship is not always one-to-one. There are major differences between Grimes's approach and the present one, however, and they can be attributed at least in part to the difference in purpose between the two investigations. For Grimes the main aim, apparently, is a study of discourse in many languages for its own sake. By contrast, the present orientation is to English primarily, to written discourse, and for ultimate application to psycholinguistic research. For this latter purpose at least, the present approach has two major advantages. The first is that it provides a systematic treatment of inferences, surely indispensible in any system that promises applications to cognition. The second advantage involves the degree of formalization in the analysis. Most of the time Grimes utilizes a "successive" exposition, discussing different aspects of discourse in successive chapters. This volume attempts to formulate unifying principles of greater generality, especially by focusing more pointedly on the text level and by taking coherence to be fundamental. Each application section has a "simultaneous" organization, in that all aspects of the analysis are embodied together in the actual representation of the structure. Thus, in this book a greater attempt has been made to fashion a wholistic text representation from the theory, although it is certainly true that selected features of Grimes's system do lend themselves to psychological research (Meyer, 1975). Recently, a comprehensive linguistic treatment of cohesion in English has been developed (Halliday & Hasan, 1976), covering the following forms of cohesion: reference, substitution, ellipsis, conjunction, and lexical cohesion. By contrast, a main theme of the present work is that an additional major source of coherence in many texts consists of the implicit propositions that can be inferred, either logically or plausibly, to bind the explicit text together. A number of other linguists have analyzed individual aspects of discourse structure without attempting an integrated theory, for example Chafe (1972) and Sanders (1970).

An approach to text grammar and description that emphasizes the natural language logic of a text is due to van Dijk (1972, 1973, 1976). He illustrates a formal derivation of a text structure (1973, pp. 66-72) based upon the notions of logical consequence, semantic consequence, and lexical meaning postulates. However, neither proposition inferences nor text hierarchies (other than macrostructures for narrative texts) are included in the representation.

Another system, one that has been productive experimentally, is Frederiksen's (1975b). Except for the analysis of logical and causal relations, however, the theory is formulated at the semantic rather than textual level. Neither text inference nor the principle of coherence is prominent in the approach. Besides a text's semantic structure, the other focus is on an analysis of the semantic transformations between an input text and a subject's output in the form of a recall protocol. In short, the emphasis on the semantic level and on recall transformations complements the text level focus and the projected experimental application of the present theory.

As for experimental psychological research on text comprehension, the usual strategy has been to develop a few aspects of text analysis in lieu of a full theory, in order to concentrate on experimental hypotheses and process models. For example, Kintsch's method of decomposing a text into propositions (Kintsch, 1974, 1976; Kintsch, Kozminsky, Streby, McKoon, & Keenan, 1975) is useful both in the selection of experimental materials and in the analysis of data. Similar comments apply to Meyer's (1975) application of elements of Gimes's theory.

One way of classifying the experimental studies of comprehension and memory is according to which aspects of text structure identified by the present theory are investigated. To mention just some of the experiments, Kieras (1967) has studied reference, while a number of researchers have examined implication (e.g., Bransford, Barclay, & Franks, 1972; Brockway, Chmielewski, & Cofer, 1974; Frederiksen, 1975a; Keenan & Kintsch, 1974; Paris & Upton, 1976; Thorndyke, 1976). Text segmentation has been studied by Koen, Becker, and Young (1969). Various studies of text levels and hierarchies have been reported (e.g., Crothers, 1972; Frase, 1969; Johnson, 1970; Kintsch & Keenan, 1974; Meyer & McConkie, 1973). Among the studies of the role of the more thematic levels of the hierarchy, one might cite Crothers (1972), Dooling and Lachman (1971), Kintsch and van Dijk (1975), Perfetti and Goldman (1974), and Pompi and Lachman (1967). The role of new and old information has been examined by Haviland and Clark (1974). Lexical factors have been investigated too, including abstractness-concreteness (deVilliers, 1974; Yuille & Paivio, 1969) and associativity (Rosenberg, 1968).

A combination of artificial intelligence and experimental psychology is seen in Rumelhart's (1975) research on story plot structure. In addition to the hierarchic representation, attention is given to proposing principles of text summarization. Turning to the natural language understanding programs in artificial intelligence, their orientation to processes makes difficult a comparison with the present system. Major systems for text processing are being developed (Anderson, 1976; Schank, 1975b; Simmons & Slocum, 1972; Winograd, 1972). These share with the present approach an emphasis on inference, especially Rieger's (1975) inferential component of Schank's system. Otherwise the two orientations are conspicuously different, generally along the lines of text structure versus knowledge structure. But it is safe to say that the two objectives will always interact; the greater the amount of world knowledge programmed in a system, the more important is it to devise efficient general principles for exploiting that knowledge to achieve comprehension. If one guiding principle is to be a search for a coherent representation of a text, the present theory can then be said to identify those inferences that a processor must use its memory and strategies to execute.

1.4 SUMMARY

Chapter 1 has defined the basic issues confronting a text level theory and has framed the present objectives in response to those issues. It has been argued that what is needed is a descriptive theory at the text level of analysis, that such a theory requires a major component for inferences, and that the notion of text coherence is the key to a text level inferential theory. Another rationale for the theory is its prospect for application to psychological and educational experimentation in comprehension and memory; the modular architecture of the theory affords a basis for simplifying the descriptions to make such applications feasible. A survey of current approaches leads to the conclusion that despite their merits they are inadequate for the present objectives.

2. The Theory and Some Descriptive Statistical Comparisons

2.1 INTRODUCTION

This chapter will present general principles formulated to meet the objectives set forth in Chapter 1 by proposing definitions and classifications of text inferences and other derivational operations. The full underlying text structures that these principles produce will be derived in Chapters 4-7 for the first four passages to be analyzed, following the theoretical supplement in Chapter 3. Besides introducing the principles, the other purpose of this chapter is to give a statistical summary, in the form of frequency tabulations, of the outcomes of these four applications. The statistical summary of the applications is presented in the same chapter as the general theory in order to impart a measure of the utility of the principles, both in terms of their average frequency of application across passages and their frequency variation from one passage to another. The statistical comparisons demonstrate the power of the theory for translating the apparently haphazard diversity of paragraph styles into an orderly pattern of structural similarities and dissimilarities.

2.2 THE FOUR PASSAGES TO BE ANALYZED IN FULL

These brief text passages will occupy our attention from the outset, because even though they will not be analyzed in detail until the latter chapters, they will nevertheless furnish many of the examples to illuminate the exposition of the theory. The passages, with apt titles added for ease of discussion, are the *State* and *Operation* paragraphs used in Chapter 1.1, plus the following two additional brief passages.

The first passage is an excerpt from the beginning of a fast-paced popular novel by J. H. Chase (1971; previously analyzed in van Dijk, 1973, pp. 66-67):

THE LUNCHROOM

It began on a summer afternoon in July, a month of intense heat, rainless skies, and scorching, dust-laden winds.

At the junction of the Fort Scott and Nevada roads, which cuts Highway 54, the trunk road from Pittsburg (sic) to Kansas City, there stands a gas station and lunchroom bar: a shabby wooden structure with one gas pump, run by an elderly widower and his fat blonde daughter.

A dusty Packard pulled up by the lunchroom a few minutes after one o'clock. There were two men in the car: one of them was asleep.

The driver got out of the car. He felt bad. He had been drinking heavily the previous night and the heat bothered him.

He paused to look at his sleeping companion, Old Sam. Then shrugging, he went into the lunchroom, leaving Old Sam to snore in the car.

The blonde was leaning over the counter. She smiled at him.

The second passage is an argumentative paragraph abridged and edited from the collected writings of Bertrand Russell (Egner & Devonn, 1967, pp. 534-535):

HISTORY

It can be concluded that history is not a science. In a science, the causal laws are more important than the particular facts. But in history, even if causal laws can be discovered at all, the particular facts still are more important than the laws. For example, in history it has been suggested that the reason for the fact that Napoleon lost the Battle of Leipzig was that he ate a peach after the Battle of Dresden. Even if it is confirmed that this was the reason, the historical fact would still be more interesting than the law.

Except for *Operation,* each of these four passages is an excerpt from a longer text. For *State* and *History* the excerpt is somewhere in the middle of the text, while for *Lunchroom* it is the beginning (with several sentences omitted for brevity). *Operation* is taken from a set of experimental materials (Pompi & Lachman, 1967), and *History* is a slight clarification of a passage adapted from Bertrand Russell for a memory experiment by Keenan and Kintsch (1974). The fact that the passages are excerpts admittedly affects the analysis somewhat, especially since some of the information that must be inferred is undoubtedly introduced in the text portion preceding the excerpt. This fact does not alter the theoretical principles, however, because any text always has some body of knowledge presumed in advance. Besides these four passages, a partial analysis of a version of the well-known *Cirlce Island* passage will be given in Chapter 8.

2.3 DEFINITIONS AND FREQUENCY COMPARISONS

We will consider two major analyses, the one of inferences and the other of the explicit text itself. Each analysis is developed around a proposed classification of different dimensions of text structure.

2.3.1 Inferences.

The analysis of inferences embraces propositional connectives and the text hierarchy, full propositions, and elements of propositions. Before introducing the detailed classification, however, a simple overview of the balance between explicit and implicit propositions in each passage is of interest. In Table 2.1, frequencies per passage are tabulated for explicit and implicit propositions and for propositional connectives. It should be emphasized that this or any count of proposition frequencies is dependent on the method of counting. A further decomposition into syntactically more elementary propositions would increase the totals, but more important for our purposes it would not greatly affect the balance between explicit and implicit propositions. In addition to the absolute counts, frequencies relative to the number of explicit propositions in the passage have been adjoined, in order to compensate for the differences in passage lengths.

Table 2.1   Propositions and Connectives: Absolute and Relative Frequencies[a]

	State	Lunchroom	History	Operation
Propositions:				
Explicit	16	29	17	15
Inferred or Parallels	4	6	33	30
Total Propositions	20 (1.25)	35 (1.21)	50 (2.94)	45 (3.00)
Connectives:[b]				
Explicit	9 (0.56)	6 (0.21)	13 (0.76)	7 (0.47)
Inferred, for Explicit Propositions	6	22	3	6
Inferred, for Inferred Propositions	4	6	33	31
Total Inferred	10 (0.62)	28 (0.97)	36 (2.12)	37 (2.47)
Total Connectives	19	34[c]	49	44

[a] Relative frequencies (in parentheses) are relative to the number of explicit propositions in that passage.
[b] Total connectives = total propositions − 1. Also, total inferred connectives = total inferred propositions + total inferred connectives joining two explicit propositions.
[c] Excludes 3 cross-hierarchic connections (see Fig. 5.1).

The main suggestion in Table 2.1 is that the analysis reveals striking structural differences among the passages. The table is arranged so that reading from left to right (in the order *State, Lunchroom, History,* and *Operation*) corresponds roughly to going from the more explicit to the more implicit passages. Specifically, *State* and *Lunchroom* have many more explicit than implicit propositions according to the analysis, while the reverse is true for *History* and *Operation.* As for connectives between propositions, even when one discounts those that connect only to implicit propositions, clear differences among the passages remain. The ratio of explicit connectives to explicit propositions is found to range from a high of 0.76 in *History* to a low of only 0.21 in *Lunchroom.* Thus, *Operation* is relatively implicit with respect to both propositions and connectives. *History* is fairly implicit with respect to propositions but explicit as to connectives. *Lunchroom,* and to some extent *State,* is the reverse of this.

Of course, to stop with this overview would be to present only a superficial description of the structures. What is needed is a taxonomy of the exact types of inferences for each passage—a classification that goes beyond proposition inferences to include element inferences as well. Tables 2.2 and 2.3 present this classification for propositions and elements of propositions, respectively. (For connectives the classification is deferred to Chapter 3.3). These two tables constitute the proposed taxonomy of inference types and, additionally, display the particular occurrence frequencies that happen to characterize the present sample of four brief passages.

Inferences of propositions. Before expounding on the classification itself, it should be observed (see Table 2.2) that the inference frequencies have been recalculated in a different, more conservative way than in Table 2.1. Now each single inference, not each proposition, is counted as a unit. In general, a single inferred antecedent or consequent can contain several elementary propositions. Nevertheless, even with the more conservative calculation, the proposition inferences remain significant from the standpoint of their overall frequency of occurrence; combined over passages the ratio of unitary inferences to explicit propositions is 0.34. The recalculated frequencies also bear out the original counts in Table 2.1 in that they vary widely across passages, from 0.73 in *Operation* to none in *State.* Now consider the classification of proposition inferences as shown in the rows of the table. Each type will be defined and exemplified, as follows:

Implication is the general term we will use here to include presuppositions, premises, and consequents. Note that implication is thus not being restricted to its conventional logical, as opposed to semantic, meaning. The reason for seeking any one term at all is to contrast these three categories with purely referential inference of propositions. Of the two main types of inferences of entire pro-

Table 2.2 Inference of Propositions: Absolute and Relative Frequencies[a,b]

	State	Lunchroom	History	Operation	Total
Proposition Inferences[c]					
Implication[d]					
A priori: Presup.[e]	0 (0)	1 (0.03)	0 (0)	2 (0.13)	3 (0.04)
A priori: Prem.	0 (0)	0 (0)	3 (0.18)	2 (0.13)	5 (0.07)
A posteriori: Presup. &					
Conseq.	0 (0)	3 (0.10)	0 (0)	1 (0.07)	4 (0.05)
A posteriori: Prem. &					
Conseq.	0 (0)	2 (0.07)	2 (0.11)	5 (0.33)	9 (0.12)
A posteriori: Conseq.	0 (0)	0 (0)	0 (0)	1 (0.07)	1 (0.01)
Total Implication	0 (0)	6 (0.20)	5 (0.29)	11 (0.73)	22 (0.29)
Reference					
A priori: Presup. Antec.	0 (0)	0 (0)	0 (0)	0 (0)	0 (0)
of Demon. Pro.					
A priori: Presup. Antec.	0 (0)	0 (0)	0 (0)	0 (0)	0 (0)
of Def. Red. NP					
A posteriori: Antec.	0 (0)	0 (0)	1 (0.06)	0 (0)	1 (0.01)
of Demon. Pro.					
A posteriori: Antec.	0 (0)	0 (0)	3 (0.18)	0 (0)	3 (0.04)
of Def. Red. NP					
Total Reference	0 (0)	0 (0)	4 (0.24)	0 (0)	4 (0.05)
Total Proposition Inferences	0 (0)	6 (0.20)	9 (0.53)	11 (0.73)	26 (0.34)

[a] Number of separate inference groups, not number of propositions inferred. Each inference group may include several propositions. The tally by number of propositions was given in Table 2.1.
[b] Relative frequencies are relative to the number of explicit propositions, given in Table 2.1.
[c] The type called *Parallels* is classified under *Regularizations*, in Table 2.4.
[d] Pooled over the three subtypes, namely possible, probable, and necessary implication.
[e] Presuppositions recoverable purely from the lexicon and syntax are too numerous and obvious to list.

positions, the implicational type is ordinarily more interesting and more frequent than the referential. Obviously, this is because most of the interesting referential inferences are of elements rather than of entire propositions.

The two kinds of implications (and the two kinds of referential inferences) will be called *a priori* and *a posteriori*. An implication is said to be *a posterori* (in relation to the passage being analyzed) if it is itself derivable as a consequent of the passage, in particular that portion of the text preceding the place at which the inference could potentially be made (anaphoric inference). For the present passages we need not be concerned with the case in which the pro-form or the like precedes its antecedent (cataphoric inference). Otherwise, the inference is *a priori*, that is, drawn from background knowledge external to the text. (This agrees with the distinction between *endophoric* and *exophoric* reference in Halliday & Hasan, 1976). The *a posteriori* type contributes to text cohesion. The *a priori* type ties the text to background knowledge. Often the *a priori*

Table 2.3 Inferences of Elements of Propositions: Absolute and Relative Frequencies

	State	Lunchroom	History	Operation	Total
Elements of Propositions:					
A priori					
Presup. Antec. Pro.	6 (0.38)	1 (0.03)	0 (0)	0 (0)	7 (0.09)
Presup. Antec. Red. NP	0 (0)	0 (0)	0 (0)	2 (0.13)	2 (0.03)
Presup. Antec. Gener. NP	0 (0)	0 (0)	0 (0)	2 (0.13)	2 (0.03)
Presup. Antec. Def. Descr. NP	0 (0)	0 (0)	0 (0)	0 (0)	0 (0)
Presup. Verb, Adverb	0 (0)	0 (0)	1 (0.06)	2 (0.13)	3 (0.04)
Presup. Case	2 (0.13)	2 (0.07)	0 (0)	1 (0.07)	5 (0.07)
Total *A priori*	8 (0.51)	3 (0.10)	1 (0.06)	7 (0.47)	19 (0.25)
A posteriori					
Antec. Pro.	10 (0.63)	9 (0.31)	1 (0.06)	4 (0.27)	24 (0.32)
Antec. Red. NP	0 (0)	6 (0.21)	4 (0.24)	2 (0.13)	12 (0.16)
Antec. Gener. NP	0 (0)	3 (0.10)	0 (0)	0 (0)	3 (0.04)
Antec. Def. Descr. NP	0 (0)	2 (0.06)	0 (0)	0 (0)	2 (0.03)
Verb, Adverb	0 (0)	0 (0)	0 (0)	0 (0)	0 (0)
Case	0 (0)	0 (0)	1 (0.06)	7 (0.47)	8 (0.11)
Total *A posteriori*	10 (0.63)	20 (0.69)	6 (0.35)	13 (0.87)	49 (0.64)
Total Elements of Propositions	18 (1.13)	23 (0.79)	7 (0.41)	20 (1.33)	68 (0.89)

type also contributes in its own way to cohesion; for example, two propositions can cohere by virtue of being jointly a conclusion from an *a priori* premise.

Consider first presuppositions, beginning with *a priori* presuppositions. A presupposition of a statement X is, following standard usage, another statement Y such that both X and its negation entail Y. For example, in *Operation* the statements *Chief Resident Jones adjusted (did not adjust) his face mask* both entail the existence of Chief Resident Jones and his face mask. Hence the affirmation, and likewise the negation, presupposes these two particular existences. Presuppositions of existence are clearly too numerous and obvious to be worth tabulating in the theoretical description. Nor have the general conversational postulates (Grice, 1975) been listed—for example, that the reader does not already know the full content of the passage. Quite different from these are any presupposed topics, which, being topical, are an important part of a description whenever they are inferable. Again, in *Operation,* both the affirmation and the negation *Chief Resident Jones adjusted (did not adjust) his face mask while anxiously surveying a pale figure secured to the long gleaming table* entail that a medical operation is about to begin. But nowhere in the paragraph is the allusion to a medical operation made explicit. Hence, in relation to the paragraph this presupposition is *a priori*.

The other subtype of presupposition is abbreviated *Presup. & Conseq.* This is the *a posteriori* type; here there is a proposition that is simultaneously presupposed in a later part of the text and derivable from an earlier part. An example arises in *Lunchroom: A dusty Packard pulled up by the lunchroom.* The more commonplace situation, which is not the case here, would be if the inference *A Packard was dusty* were simply a routine existential presupposition as discussed above. However, this time it happens that this inference is itself a (possible) consequent of an earlier part of the text, namely the first sentence: *It began on a summer afternoon in July, a month of . . . and scorching dust-laden winds.* The reason this evidently infrequent sort of inference is worth noting is that it does contribute to the text coherence.

Just as there are these two subtypes of presuppositions, so too are there two corresponding subtypes of premises. A premise is, of course, an antecedent that is assumed rather than presupposed. Its consequent follows either by semantic possibility or probability or by logical necessity.

The first subtype of premise, the *a priori,* is abbreviated *Prem.* This subtype poses the same general theoretical problem as did *Presup.* The inference is by definition connected to the text on only one end; within the text it is an antecedent but not a consequent. Being less constrained by the text, then, the pure premises threaten to grow unmanageably numerous. Often one can conceive of a wealth of antecedent conditions for the text propositions; what is less simple is to devise a criterion for keeping the number of formally represented antecedents to a manageable minimum. Although this important issue requires further study, a tentative resolution of it can be suggested. Three conditions bear on the decision as to whether or not to include the premise: (1) if it is needed as one of the premises in an argument, (e.g., by *modus ponens* or *modus tollens);* (2) if it is simply the sole premise for a statement, then the more propositions it unites by serving as their joint premise, the stronger is the case for including that premise in the representation; and (3) conceivably, some prospective antecedents might be inconsequential by the structural criteria, but nonetheless worth including on the grounds that they are subjectively compelling. At least when psychological applications of the theory are contemplated, it might be a mistake to exclude such inferable premises. But however the question of criteria should ultimately be decided, the applications to five passages included in this book rely chiefly on the first criterion, the role of the premise in an argument. Only one of the pure premise inferences resorts to the other criteria alone, namely in *History.* Here the inferable premise *In a science, the causal laws are more general than the particular facts* serves to rationalize the explicit statement *In a science, the causal laws are more important than the particular facts. History* also points up an example of a minor inferable premise disregarded because it fails the first two criteria: *The reason Napoleon lost the Battle of Leipzig was that (since he was hungry and a peach was available) he ate a peach after the Battle of Dresden,* in which the potential inference is parenthesized. Admittedly, what is trite or insignificant to one reader might be salient to another, so the invoking of the salience criterion would force one somehow to handle such inferences.

The *a posteriori* type of premise, abbreviated *Prem. & Conseq.,* is by definition joined to the text on both the antecedent and consequent ends. Hence, in this case there would appear to be little danger of a proliferation of inferences. Like *Presup. & Conseq.*, its premise counterpart is important for enhancing the cohesion of the text. The difference, obviously, is that now *Prem. & Conseq.* inferences function to explicate any assumed intermediate steps between stated antecedent and stated consequent. The simplest situation is when only one such intervening step need be inferred, and moreover the propositions it mediates are immediately adjacent in the surface text. Either of these conditions can fail; that is, in some texts several intermediate inferences are needed or propositions irrelevant to the argument are confusing interposed between premise and conclusion. Interesting examples of *Prem. & Conseq.* are by no means rare in the sample of texts. Again taking an example from *History*, there is the inference *If history were a science, then in history the causal laws would be more important than the particular facts.* This is first a consequent of the stated *In a science, the causal laws are more important that the particular facts.* In turn, it is also one of the premises for the stated conclusion *It can be concluded that history is not a science.* Among the more notable examples to be encountered in later chapters are one involving transitivity and another in which premises are invoked to derive a presupposition.

The remaining possibility for an implicational inference of a proposition is one that is simply a consequent in relation to the text; this type is abbreviated *Conseq.* The situation is symmetrical to that for *Prem.* but this time the inference is connected to the text on only the consequent end. Therefore, again the same potential exists for a proliferation of tangential inferences. To curtail them the same criteria again apply. In practice, criterion (2) has proven useful: the more propositions of the text that the prospective inferred consequent unites by serving as their joint consequent, the stronger the case is for including it in the representation. The extreme instance, of course, is a consequent theme inferred for an entire passage. In fact, exactly this occurs in *Operation*, where after some preliminary inferences there is a culminating inference: *Chief Resident Jones' operation on the pale figure did not accomplish the point.* This phrase confers the coherence lacking in the explicit text, which narrates the individual episodes but then leaves their outcome to the reader. The significance of this type of inference in comprehension makes up for its rarity in our sample. This completes the main part of the classification of proposition inferences, the implicational ones.

The entire classification of proposition inferences would be incomplete without commenting on the purely referential inferences of propositions. Their referential role is the same as the one more typically played by element inferences. The subtypes presently suggested appear in the bottom half of Table 2.2; there may be others as well. Such inferences are usually routine and perhaps infrequent, and hence can be disposed of quickly. All four present examples come from *History*. The first comes shortly after the explicit lines *it has been suggested that the reason Napoleon lost the Battle of Leipzig was that he ate a peach after the Battle of Dresden,* there occurs *Even if it is confirmed that the reason was this* . . . . The latter phrase contains two terms whose antecedents are to be found in the former; obviously, *the reason* refers to *the reason Napoleon lost the Battle of Leipzig,* and the demonstrative pronoun *this* has the phrase *that he ate a peach after the Battle of Dresden* as its antecedent. Such reduced surface forms help achieve a crisp style by avoiding tedious repetition of lengthy subordinate clauses. In both instances the understood antecedent is a nominalized proposition, and thus is ultimately a full proposition rather than only an element of one.

Inferences of elements of propositions. Under this heading we will group all inferences such that part of the proposition is explicit, part implicit in the surface sentence. (See Table 2.3.) A basic issue arises here. Whether or not all such inferences are for reference—that is, for identifying the situation being referred to—depends on how broadly one construes the notion of reference. If it is restricted to coreference—to identifying individuals by recovering antecedents of pronouns and the like—then there are element inferences that are not referential in this sense. An example is inference of understood noun phrases to fill empty semantic case slots. On the other hand, if reference is viewed more broadly as encompassing not only individual coreference but event reference as well, then all element inferences are referential in this broader sense. This broader view will be adopted here. An important consequence of not limiting reference to coreference is that it also allows into the formulation the phenomenon of non-coreferential inference of individuals. *Lunchroom* offers some examples, including the parenthesized inference in *The blonde was leaning over the counter (of the lunchroom).* Here *lunchroom* but not *counter* was introduced previously in the text. Clearly, the inference is referential; it identifies which counter is meant. Equally clearly, *counter* is "part-referential" to, rather than coreferential with, *lunchroom.* In short, then, the classification of referential inferences of propositional elements reveals a diversity of subtypes ranging from the trivial to the significant.

Before proceeding to the classification, note the occurrence frequencies summed over our passages in the right-hand column of Table 2.3. Collectively, referential inferences are notable for their high frequency of occurrence; the ratio of such inferences to the total number of explicit propositions over all four passages is 0.89. Separately, however, most of the individual subtypes other than pronominalization are rather infrequent. But the number of inference subtypes is large, and their very rarity can impede understanding of their proper theoretical analysis. Hence, any useful typology must include even the infrequent subtypes.

Again, besides the frequencies over all paragraphs, the other instructive aspect of Table 2.3 is the comparative one, and again it reveals sharp differences among the four passages. The ordering is not the same as that already noted in Table 2.2 for proposition inferences. Although *Operation* again leads with the highest relative frequency of element inferences, now *State* is second highest, while *History* becomes the lowest. Thus there can be, but does not have to be, a tradeoff between the relative frequencies of proposition and element inferences.

Now consider the classification shown in Table 2.3. All element inferences are for reference. The table excludes the transparently simple, routine case of coreference by lexical identity plus a shift from indefinite to definite article. Within reference the primary division is between the *a priori* and the *a posteriori* types, just as it was for proposition inference. Consistent with the definitions given there, a referential inference is *a posteriori* (again, in relation to the text being analyzed) if the antecedent occurs earlier in the text, and *a priori* if it does not. The *a posteriori* type is the more prevalent one in the sample, no doubt because the *a priori* subtype tends to be limited more to the beginning of a passage. Under each of the two main types are subsumed the same six subtypes, those listed in Table 2.3. The following definitions and examples exhibit this variety of linguistic resources for conveying reference.

Let us begin with *a priori* subtypes. In Table 2.3 they have been labelled *Presup. Antec.*, followed by the name of the anaphor (e.g., *Presup. Antec. Pro.* for a presupposed antecedent of a pronoun). The label *Presup.* reflects the fact than an *a priori* referential inference is a presupposition in relation to the entire text being analyzed. By contrast, an *a posteriori* referential inference has its antecedent explicit somewhere earlier in the text (though of course that antecedent is also presupposed relative only to the particular sentence containing the anaphor).

A presupposed antecedent of a pronoun, denoted *Presup. Antec. Pro.*, occurs in the first sentence of *State: I saw that the state was half-witted . . . .* In relation to the excerpt there has not been a previous introduction of the antecedent of the pronoun *I* (nor could there have been, since *I* is the first word of the excerpt). The presupposed antecedent is obviously Thoreau, the author of the passage.

A presupposed antecedent of a reduced noun phrase, denoted *Presup. Antec. Red. NP,* differs in that deletion rather than pronominalization is what produces the anaphor from the antecedent. Usually, perhaps always, what is deleted is a modifier. For example, in the context of *Operation* the stated NP *a pale figure* is inferred to be an anaphor derived by modifier deletion from the antecedent *a pale human figure,* though *human* is never explicit. Note that in this subtype the anaphor can have an indefinite article.

A presupposed antecedent of a generic noun phrase, *Presup. Antec. Gener. NP,* is similar except that the antecedent is inferred by lexical substitution of a specific member of the generic category, instead of by recovering deleted words. Again citing *Operation,* the noun phrase *small sharp instrument* contains the generic noun *instrument,* whose inferred antecedent is *knife* (or perhaps *scalpel*), making *small sharp knife* the inferred antecedent.

A presupposed antecedent of a definite descriptive noun phrase, *Presup. Antec. Def. Descr. NP,* differs in that the anaphor is a nominalized verb rather than a generic noun. Although no examples of this subtype occur in these four passages, it is clear what they would be from their *a posteriori* counterpart, which does occur. One of the few instances of this counterpart is in *Lunchroom,* namely the definite descriptive anaphor *the driver,* which consists of the definite article followed by the nominalized form of the verb *drive.* In context, the antecedent turns out to be *the other of the two men.* The corresponding *a priori* example, then, would be an excerpt from *Lunchroom,* beginning with the sentence containing the anaphor. Another example would be a text beginning with *The winner of the 1976 U.S. presidential election.*

The remaining two subtypes of *a priori* element inference, as well as of course their counterparts for *a posteriori* inference, are those having to do with the identification of events rather than of individuals. An inference of a presupposed verb or adverb, denoted *Presup. Verb* or *Presup. Adverb,* identifies the event being referred to. One of the few examples comes from *History,* specifically the elliptical NP *the Battle of Dresden* in *Napoleon lost the Battle of Leipzig because he ate a peach after the Battle of Dresden.* Surely one would readily infer the verb *fought,* or perhaps even *won,* yielding the inference *after the Battle of Dresden (was fought).* Inference of a presupposed entry in a semantic case slot, *Presup. Case,* completes the expansion of the same elliptical NP. Here the probable agent is inferred to be Napoleon, so with both inferences supplied the reading is *Napoleon lost the Battle of Leipzig because he ate a peach after (he fought) the Battle of Dresden.* Of course, there is no particular reason why verb and case inferences have to go together, and in general they do not. As shown in Table 2.3, the number of semantically significant inferences of presupposed cases is quite small in our sample of passages.

Turning now to the lower half of the table, these same six subtypes recur for *a posteriori* inference:

An antecedent of a pronoun, *Antec. Pro.,* is usually quite routine. Examples from *Lunchroom* are the pronouns in *She smiled at him,* whose respective antecedents *The elderly widower's fat blonde daughter* and *the driver* have already been introduced in the text. Occasionally such inferences are more interesting, especially when a text either creates ambiguity between two possible antecedents or else interposes many sentences between the antecedent and its subsequent pronominal anaphor. Owing to their high frequency in *State,* inferences of pronoun antecedents are by far the most frequent subtype of *a posteriori* inference in the sample.

An antecedent of a reduced noun phrase, *Antec. Red. NP,* is more interesting. Being *a posteriori,* the anaphor is normally preceded by the definite article. Both coreferential and noncoreferential variants occur. An example of the first is the anaphor *the laws* in *History,* reduced from its intended antecedent *the causal laws.* An example of the second occurs in *Lunchroom,* in which context *the previous night* is reduced from *the night previous to the summer afternoon in July.* Here the inferred antecedent, *a summer afternoon in July,* is introduced before, but is not coreferential with, the anaphor. If the syntactic generalization suggested by these examples is valid, the anaphor is coreferential or noncoreferential with its antecedent according to whether the deleted phrase is prenominal or postnominal, respectively.

An antecedent of a generic noun phrase, *Antec. Gener. NP,* is ordinarily a straightforward subtype. If the anaphor is definite, then anaphor and antecedent are coreferential. An example is the anaphor *the car* in *Lunchroom,* whose antecedent *A dusty Packard* was already introduced. The noncoreferential variant would obviously begin with a different article (e.g., that in *another car*). In principle, though probably seldom in practice, the inference could be a difficult one: a reader might not recognize the generic category to which the antecedent belongs.

An antecedent of a descriptive noun phrase, *Antec. Def. Descr. NP.,* requires some discussion. Recall that according to our treatment the NP in this subtype is a nominalized verb rather than a true noun. The only two examples found in the sample are the anaphors *the driver* from the verb *drive* and *his companion* from *accompany,* both in *Lunchroom.* The eligible antecedents previously introduced are *two men* and *the one of the two men.* The latter turns out to be coreferential with *his companion,* so for it no problem of classification arises. But for *the driver* the analysis is more involved. If one insists on an explicit antecedent, then it can only be the remaining candidate, namely *two men,* in relation to which *the driver (of the two men)* is noncoreferential. But if one is willing to allow implicit antecedents, it then turns out that a proposition containing *the other of the two men* can be derived, which antecedent is the coreferential one sought for the definite anaphor *the driver.* As will be explained in Chapter 5.2.1, the reason this duality of antecedent arises is inherent in the proposed treatment of definite descriptions, which in fact differs from that for other anaphors. Only for definite descriptions have entire propositions asserting coreference (e.g., *The other of the two men was the driver*) been formally inferred. The reason is that for the other subtypes the coreference is obvious. Using pronouns as an example, it is totally unnecessary to formalize *She was the blonde* in order to mark the fact that the antecedent of *She* in *She smiled at him* is *a blonde* previously introduced. After all, every blonde is a she, every Packard is a car, and so forth, but not every man is a driver. For the theory in general, however, it is certainly conceivable that, say in a mystery novel or a freshman composition, some other subtype of anaphor might also require nontrivial proposition inferences in order to establish an antecedent.

An *a posteriori* verb inference, denoted simply *Verb,* differs in the obvious way from the *a priori* inference just discussed. No examples arise in the passages. The corresponding example would be if *the Battle of Dresden was fought* had occurred explicitly preceding the anaphor *the Battle of Dresden* that did occur.

An *a posteriori* inference of an entry in a semantic case slot, *Case*, is a moderately frequent subtype. Nearly all of the present occurrences are in *Operation*. For example, after *the opening* has been introduced as being *in the skin of the pale figure*, one can infer the locative case in *another aide pushed aside glistening surface fat (from the opening);* this also occurs in *vital parts were laid bare (inside the opening).* These inferences make up for the failure of the surface text to say that the fat, vital parts, and so on, are organically part of the pale figure. Also with texts in general one would wish to avoid a plethora of trivial inferences. One possible criterion for their inclusion could be that the potential inference differ in some way from the antecedent—that is, that it shift the semantic case or at least the preposition. Another criterion might be that several other propositions intervene between antecedent case and its inferred recurrence.

With this subtype the classification of element inferences is completed, thus concluding our discussion of the entire typology of inferences.

2.3.2 Other derivations.

Although the principal concern of this book is inference, a complete description would include an analysis of the explicit text itself. (See Table 2.4.) Such an analysis would not be properly classed with inference, however. Granted, in the broadest possible sense of the word "inference," any description that goes beyond the literal text is an inference. But in the stricter sense, an interpretation qualifies as an inference only if it adds to the text representation, not if it characterizes it abstractly. Therefore, the perception that a text contains abstract words, say, or that two of its words are synonyms, or that a text expression is a metaphor, comes under the present heading rather than under the heading of inferences. As shown in Table 2.4, beyond inferences the three classes of text properties included in the present description are what will be called *regularizations, categorizations,* and *figurative interpretations.* Entire theories devoted essentially to each of these could be developed in their own right, but at present we will aim more modestly, at describing these text properties.

Regularizations. This term will be used for those operations whose function is to render a text's structure more internally consistent and symmetrical. Regularizing differs in an important way from explicating; it probably makes little difference whether the underlying structure is taken to be the postregularization structure, as has been done here, or whether instead the regularizations are viewed merely as optional side commentary on the preregularization underlying structure. Too, regularization should not be confused with text editing, one

Table 2.4 Regularizations, Categorizations, and Figurative Interpretations: Absolute and Relative Frequencies[a]

	State	Lunchroom	History	Operation	Total
Regularizations					
Propositions (Parallel)	2 (0.13)	0 (0)	1 (0.06)	3 (0.20)	6 (0.08)
Element of Proposition	3 (0.19)	0 (0)	1 (0.06)	3 (0.20)	7 (0.09)
Order of Propositions	2 (0.13)	0 (0)	1 (0.06)	0 (0)	3 (0.04)
Total Regularizations	7 (0.45)	0 (0)	3 (0.18)	6 (0.40)	16 (0.21)
Categorizations[b]					
Spatial, temporal	0	+	0	0	
Animate	+	+	+	+	
Action, being	+	+	+	+	
Manner	0	0	0	+	
Inanimate, concrete	0	+	+	+	
Inanimate, abstract	+	0	+	0	
Regualtions, Intracategory					
Identity	0	7	7	0	14 (0.18)
Set Inclusion	0	5	1	0	6 (0.08)
Synonymy	1	1	0	1	3 (0.04)
Antonymy, Hyponymy	7	5	9	3	24 (0.32)
Total Relations, Intra-category	8 (0.50)	18 (0.62)	17 (1.00)	4 (0.27)	47 (0.62)
Figurative Interpretations					
Metaphor, Simile	6 (0.38)	0 (0)	0 (0)	0 (0)	6 (0.08)
Total	21 (1.33)	18 (0.62)	20 (1.18)	10 (0.67)	69 (0.91)

[a] Relative frequencies are relative to the number of explicit propositions, given in Table 2.1.
[b] A "+" denotes at least a moderate number of category exemplars in the passage, and a "0" denotes none or a negligible number.

purpose of which is to remove any semantic or logical contradictions in a text. Editing is, of course, a major topic in its own right, a topic outside the scope of this volume, as mentioned in Chapter 1.2. In contrast to editing, regularization removes only inconsistencies in text style, not in content. As with other derivational operations, the identification of regularizations does not imply a commitment to any particular psychological hypothesis, either the hypothesis that they clarify the text or, oppositely, the hypothesis that they stultify it. The aim again is purely methodological, one of formulating the opportunities for regularization so that any such hypotheses may be tested. If the present sample of passages is any indication, regularizations occur with moderate frequency, though less frequently than proposition inferences.

Under regularization the first subtype is labelled *Regularization of Propositions,* also called *(Analogical) Parallel.* This kind of regularization produces a full proposition where there was none in the surface text. Hence, it might be argued that this derivational operation is misclassified, and belongs instead under proposition inferences. Perhaps so. A parallel insertion is done for the sake of symmetry, so the classification depends on which aspect—the insertion or the symmetry—is taken as the basis for the classification. *History* offers an example. The explicit conclusion of the passage is prefaced by a performative *It can be concluded* (plus its complementive subordinating connective *that*). But later the argument follows directly, without its parallel performative *It can be argued.* Hence, one can routinely insert the parallel through the analogy of *performative for conclusion: conclusion:: performative for argument: argument.* In general, one would expect occasionally to encounter more significant sorts of missing parallels. In particular, major errors of omission in a text's development might be revealed, such as the absence of parallel evidence for a counterargument in the context of presented evidence for an argument. Hence, the present examples are quite limited, namely to the detection of only those missing parallels whose insertion is largely a formality. The *Circle Island* analysis in Chapter 8 will show that in some texts parallelism is central to the development.

The next possibility, following the treatment of inferences, is *Regularization of an Element of a Proposition.* Unlike the preceding subtype, no insertion is performed here. This regularization is merely a morpho-syntactic rewriting intended to transfer a text element from one syntactic form class and semantic category to another. Again, the rationale is to increase the stylistic uniformity of the text. For example, in *State* one of the regularizations converts *I lost . . . respect for the state, and pitied it* to *I lost . . . respect for the state and had* (or *gained*) *pity for it.* The purpose of the verb-to-noun regularization of *pitied* as *pity* is fairly obvious: the author's intended contrast is heightened if both contrasting terms are placed in the same text category (here, abstract mental states) rather than left in different categories (here, a mental state and an action). Similarly, a regularization can apply to a semantic identity as well as to a contrast. An example in *History* converts the adjectival construction *the historical laws* to the nominal construction *in history, the laws* in the context of the identical previous locution *in history, the laws.* Element regularizations are tedious in the analysis. If overdone in the surface text they would be monotonous there as well. They do serve a purpose, however, and that is to highlight contrasts and identities. The more the lexically related words in a text can be transferred to the same text category, the more the search for important lexical relations can be narrowed down from the entire text to members of the same category.

The remaining subtype is called *Regularization of the Order of Propositions.* As the name implies, this regularization can apply whenever the same or corresponding propositions recur in a text, but for stylistic purposes their sequence has been varied. Here too the regularization undoes the stylistic variation. One of the few examples is in *State*, in which the original *Thus the state never intentionally confronts a man's sense, intellectual or moral, but only his body, his senses* is permuted to invert the subordination of the last two clauses, yielding . . . *his senses, his body.* For better or worse, the regularization achieved is that *sense* and *senses* are now more sharply contrasted, by being on a par syntactically. (On the other hand, if the author's intention was to contrast the wholistic terms *sense* and *body,* then this particular example is inappropriate).

Categorizations. Under this heading falls the within-proposition assignment of text elements to categories. The categorization of between-proposition connectives is a separate matter, to be discussed in Chapter 3.3. The major interest now lies in the explicit text, though once this has been categorized the extension to the implicit propositions can be routinely added. Other than the assignment *per se,* categorization logically has two aspects: the selection of primitive categories before the assignment, and after it the determination of how members of the same category are related to each other. These issues will be covered in turn.

Two quite different bases of categorization, the semantic and the rhetorical or textual, can perspicuously represent different facets of a text description. For brevity only the semantic basis will be displayed here for all four passages. The rhetorical basis will be illustrated only for *History* (Chapter 6.1), without intending to minimize its importance. A semantic scheme would take as its primitive categories such traditional semantic features as *action, animate, spatial location* and the like, to either a coarser or more refined depth of subcategorization. The scheme is thus semantic-feature based rather than semantic-case based. For example, recurrences of the same noun phrase would fall in the same category despite any case shifts. The scheme is also independent of an element's text role. For example, the main human characters and the supporting cast would go in the same *animate* category; likewise, in a narrative both actions taken and alternative courses only contemplated would fall together under the heading of *action.* Thus, the semantic classification does not say very much about the text *qua* text. A rhetorical classification does just what a semantic one does not, by being based on familiar categories such as *main characters, minor characters, background events, hypothetical events, performatives,* and so on.

Which classification is the more useful? For some purposes either is adequate. In the first place, the analysis of inferences did not assume any within-proposition categorization at all. Hence, it stands on its own merits and is independent of how or whether such an accompanying classificiation is proposed. One place where the two aspects interact is in the representation of referential inferences. For quick scanning of later tables it is convenient to have all referentially related terms tabulated in the same column. Both schemes apparently accommodate this requirement. Another formal condition easily met by both is that, for the sake of simplicity, the number of categories be manageably small. The other side of the coin is that, where the two taxonomic princples differ, each offers certain advantages. The semantic classification is a direct way of recording the distribution of concrete vs. abstract, animate vs. inanimate, and the like, surely an attribute of no small importance in distinguishing among texts. The rhetorical classification on the other hand is intrinsically a textual, as opposed to lexical, description. Weighing these factors, it would seem that ideally both descriptions are worth including.

A few secondary details of the semantic categorization deserve mention. The six categories adopted for the present passages are admittedly somewhat arbitrary from the standpoint of how fine a subclassification is used. Nouns undergo a moderately specific subclassification, but primarily for expedience the verbs are not subcategorized at all. Another small detail is that in the present system pro-adverbs (e.g., THEN in AND THEN) are treated as part of the connective. Consequently, the fact that AND THEN expresses a temporal relationship shows up in the classification of connectives (Chapter 3.3) rather than in the categorization of elements. In effect, AND THEN is being viewed as semantically more like IF/THEN than like, say, *AND IN 1929.*

With respect to the present four passages, Table 2.4 shows that each contains, with a nonnegligible frequency, from three to four of the six categories. No two passages contain exactly the same categories. Among the four passages three are unique with respect to one or another category: only *Lunchroom* includes a *spatial, temporal* framework, only *Operation* a *manner* category, while only *State* lacks an *inanimate, concrete* category.

Given that the primitive categories have been decided and the category assignments determined, the remaining aspect of the description of intracategory relations is the pattern of semantic and logical relations holding among cocategorized elements of different propositions. Just as the text hierarchy spells out the coherent progression of propositions, the relations specify the coherent succession of elements. The particular relations proposed are: identity (e.g., *history/history*); set inclusion (e.g., by enumeration in *an elderly widower and his fat blonde daughter/the blonde,* by quantification in *two men/one of them,* or by pluralization in *facts/fact*); synonymy (e.g., *aide/assistant*); and *antonymy* or *hyponymy* (e.g., the coordinate hyponyms *suggested* and *confirmed,* and also the noncoordinate hyponyms *car* and *Packard*).

Unfortunately, sometimes the judgment of to whether or not a semantic relation holds between two elements is necessarily tenuous. It is impractical to consult or devise an elaborate semantic atlas to resolve the matter, when all that is being sought is a simple description of one of the many facets of a text. Therefore, an expedient tactic has been resorted to—namely, settling for the subjectively more direct relations and ignoring the debatable ones. In borderline cases (e.g., *honesty* and *wit* in *State*) the last recourse is to let the text structure influence the judgment, by recognizing the prospective relationship if and only if the entire propositions in question are closely connected in the text.[1]

---

[1] Several details have to be tentatively resolved, as follows: when a category member is potentially relatable to more than one predecessor, the dominant relationship is taken to be that suggested by the text structure (e.g., in *History, facts* is deemed related to *laws* in

As for the four passages, a brief summary of the analysis is as follows: *Lunchroom* creates a "zoom" effect by several times exploiting set inclusion to narrow the focus from enumerated two-element sets to single elements (e.g., the first two examples cited above). *State* exhibits an elaborate barrage of new coordinates, *History* introduces a few identities and coordinates and then repeats them over and over, while in *Operation* the category successors are scarcely lexically related at all. For all relations combined, the relative frequency varies from a high of 1.00 in *History* to a low of 0.27 in *Operation*. Hyponymy is fairly conspicuous in three of the four passages, identity in two, set inclusion in one, and synonymy in none.

Figurative interpretations. This term covers the occurrences of metaphor, simile, and the like in a text. Here too there is no pretense that a serious theoretical treatment of the phenomenon in its own right is being attempted. Again, the aim is the more modest one of text description. The only present examples occur in *State,* in which figurative speech enlivens an abstract paragraph. Indeed, the entire development is a likening of the state to a person (e.g., *I saw that the state was half-witted . . .).* Generally speaking, such devices enhance a text's impact by relating the new to the familiar or vivid.

2.4 SUMMARY

Altogether, then, the system can be viewed in three aspects: the general theory, the statistical summary of the outcome of an application of the theory, and the structural outcome of such an application—that is to say, the derived underlying text structure. This chapter has addressed the first two aspects, leaving the actual underlying structures and their detailed derivations for Chapters 4-7 (plus the partial analysis in Chapter 8).

As to the general principles, foremost among them is the formulation of a taxonomy of text inferences. Accompanying this is a description of the explicit text. To aid in presenting the principles for describing implicit and explicit text, examples have been drawn from four passages. To exemplify the kinds of statistical summaries the theory enables, frequency tabulations of important structural characteristics have been presented for the four passages. These tabulations constitute the statistical representations of the outcomes of applying the theory, corresponding to the structural representations to be derived in Chapters 4-7.

---

the same sentence, rather than to *facts* in an earlier sentence). Other details are that pro-words are not eligible for participation in semantic relations as herein defined, that the analysis oversimplifies by excluding relations within the same proposition, and that modifiers in otherwise unrelated constructions (e.g., the participles in *gleaming table* and *glistening surface fat*) are deemed unrelated.

3. Supplements to the Theory: Text Information Newness, Logical–Semantic Connectives, and Summary

3.1 INTRODUCTION

This chapter presents three additional facets of a text's structure. These analyses are best viewed as supplements to the main description introduced in Chapter 2, because they are performed either separately from, or subsequent to, the inference of the underlying structure. The additional analyses are both less detailed and more tentative than is the treatment of inferences. What is especially attractive about these supplementary analyses is that each offers a characterization of an intuitively important text property, one that moreover can be determined fairly readily without a lengthy, detailed examination of the underlying text. The analyses do turn out to reveal additional marked differences among the sample of passages. The differences brought to light are consistent with one's subjective impressions of the passages, and therefore establish a logical-linguistic foundation for those impressions.

As in the preceding chapter, the emphasis now will be on introducing the basic notions, exemplifying them with excerpts from the passages, and presenting descriptive statistics for the applications to the four passages. Details of the complete applications will be omitted for the sake of brevity.

3.2 INFORMATION NEWNESS AND CONTRAST

A familiar impression is that surface texts can differ greatly in the rate at which they introduce new informaton as opposed to repeating old information. (Here "old" and "new" are of course defined in relation to the text, not according to our past knowledge of the information content.) Hence, this property is well worth formalizing in the description. Being intended for written texts, our treatment disregards the concept of an information block defined by intonation contours (Halliday, 1967) as a unit of textual cohesion (Grimes, 1975, Chapter 19). The present analysis will be limited to the element level, because for most of our passages there is virtually no surface repetition of entire propositions (cf. Grimes's 1975, pp. 292ff. concept of an "overlay). Also, orthogonal to the new vs. old dichotomy is the dichotomy of contrastive vs. noncontrastive element information. This, of course, bears on the analyses of intracategory relations already discussed, where it was noted that *State* and *History*, but not *Lunchroom* or *Operation,* exhibit many coordinate elements. There the aim was to ascertain which particular logical-semantic relations occurred. The difference from the present analysis is that semantic relatedness is a lexical matter, but information contrast as here conceived is a syntactic matter; the underlying structures must by syntactically parallel. Altogether, then, a two-fold classification of text information is proposed: new vs. old orthogonal to contrastive vs. noncontrastive. This treatment differs from that of Chafe (1970, p. 224), who suggests that new and contrastive information are in complementary distributions, according to whether the sentences are noncontrastive or contrastive, respectively. The present formulation allows us to classify as new the first occurrence of a contrasting pair, and as old any later recurrences of the pair. The conclusion to be drawn from the comparison presented next is that the classification does represent a significant dimension of text variation, and moreover that except for a few problematic details the analysis is fairly simple to perform.

The analysis is best explained by exemplifying it with a particular passage. It turns out that all but one of the several unresolved details arise in *Lunchroom,* hence that passage is the most appropriate one for the present discussion (see Table 3.1). Table 3.1 displays only the analysis for P16-P22, for the sake of brevity. The notation is defined in the first table footnote. First, observe that the information classification is partly independent of the exact category or column in which a text element is entered. If a second element is new in any case, it will be so designated regardless of which column it is assigned to in the table. Therefore, for our purpose it is immaterial whether or not, say, spatial terms are entered in the same column as temporal terms. What does matter, obviously, is the choice of syntactic constructions to be the units for the tabulation. Here the units have been taken to be the same as in the previously discussed tables of categorized surface text. Recall that for simplicity the unit adopted is not always an elementary one syntactically (e.g., modals have been left with verbs, and articles, prepositions, quantifiers, and prenominal adjectives with nouns).

Most of the classification would seem intuitively acceptable. For example, lexical repetition of the syntactic head of a unit counts as old information, as does it pronominalization. Contrast happens not to occur in this excerpt from

Table 3.1 Illustrative Excerpt from the Information Analysis for *Lunchroom*[a,b]

16 pulled up^n	a few minutes	by the lunch-			A dusty Packard^n
"	after one	room°			
"	o'clock^n				
17 were^n			there°; two men^n in the car°?		
18 was asleep^n			one of them°		
19 got out^n			The driver°?	of the car°	
20 felt bad^n			He°		
21 had been	the previous				
" drinking^n	night^n				heavily^n
22 bothered^n		the heat°	him°		

[a]The notation is as follows. The superscripts *n* and *o* denote new and old information, respectively. (No contrastive information happens to occur in this excerpt). A question mark "?" denotes an uncertain classification.
[b]Propositions are numbered serially, in lefthand column.

Lunchroom, but generally occurs when the two or more underlying propositions are identical except in one position. For example, the sentence *In a science the particular facts are more important than the causal laws (are important)* embodies a contrast between *the particular facts* and *the causal laws.* A contrast is viewed as symmetric, so that both corresponding elements are counted as contrasting with each other, not just the second with the first. Several other cases are less clear and do require comment:

1. For synonyms, the second of the two elements is counted as old, not new. Thus, the classification is based on meaning rather than lexicon. This is consistent with the classification of an *a posteriori* pronoun as old in relation to its antecedent.

2. A repetition—except for minor changes of an article, preposition, modifier, and so forth—is classified as old. This is also done for changes of mood, tense, number, and so on.

3. The conditions for contrast are broadened to include contrasts brought to light by element regularization, in keeping with the treatment of contrasts in the preceding chapters. Two problematic cases (denoted by question marks in Table 3.1) have so far been encountered, discussed next.

4. One uncertain detail is whether or not the definition of contrast should be broadened beyond clauses alone to include phrase level "contrasts." Examples are the two noun phrases in *its friends from its foes,* and also the two in *a gas station and lunchroom bar.* Presumably the same decision should be made regardless of how the phrases are linked, by preposition or conjunction. Tentatively, these constructions have been included among the contrasts.

5. The other uncertain detail is whether a definite descriptive NP and also a definite generic NP should be regarded as new or as old in relation to an introduced antecedent. Examples, by now familiar, include *one of them, his sleeping companion* for definite description, and *A dusty Packard* and *in the car* for generic description. For both kinds the second member of the pair is probably best classified as old in relation to the first. This accords with the classifying of an *a posteriori* pronoun as old in relation to its antecedent.

When these details are thus tentatively resolved, the resulting comparison of passages is shown in Table 3.2. Marked differences among passages emerge once again. *Operation* is mostly new element information. *History* is about half new and half old, displaying also a remarkably high proportion of element contrasts. *Lunchroom* and *State* are intermediate, but the narrative *Lunchroom* is more like the narrative *Operation;* likewise the argumentative *State* is more like the argumentative *History*. That is, *State* is higher in contrasts, lower in new information, than is *Lunchroom*. Fortunately, the general pattern in Table 3.2 is discernible despite the several problematic instances.

3.3 LOGICAL-SEMANTIC CONNECTIVES BETWEEN PROPOSITIONS

An important question is how to conceptualize the relationships that hold among propositions of a text. One interesting way of doing so is solely in semantic terms, such as *attribution, manner, specification,* and so forth (Grimes, 1975, Chapter 14). Another method can be put in terms of the natural language connections, (e.g., van Dijk, 1973). Connective analyses of the latter sort have been proposed by van Dijk (1976) and Frederiksen (1975b). The present treatment is in this vein, but differs from these two in orientation. Instead of being

Table 3.2   Proportions of each Element Information Type in each Passage

	State	Lunchroom	History	Operation
New	.42(.46?)[a]	.58(.74?)[b]	.32	.86
New, contrastive	.18(.14?)[a]	.12(.00?)[b]	.19	.00
Old	.34	.30(.26?)[b]	.30	.14
Old, contrastive	.06	.00	.19	.00

[a] If substitutions at the phrase level are counted as *New, contrastive,* then the proportions outside the parentheses are correct; otherwise, the proportions are as in parentheses.
[b] Between *New* and *New, contrastive,* see the preceding footnote; between *New* and *Old*, the proportions depend on which way definite descriptive NP's and definite generic NP's are counted.

concerned with the abstract properties of the connectives themselves, the emphasis here is on deciding which connective to infer at a given point in the surface text being analysed. Once again the analysis rests on a classification aimed at systematizing the inference-making procedure. The other main purpose of the classification, as we have said, is to furnish a basis for a quantitative comparison of the propositional connections in different texts.

Tables 3.3 and 3.4 give the classification along with one or more examples of each class. The scope of the analysis has been restricted as follows: only propositional (clausal) connectives in underlying structure, not elemental (phrasal) connectives, have been included in the representation. Also, for simplicity, all connections are assumed to have been reduced to binary ones (i.e., between a pair of propositions). Finally, negation, being an operator on the proposition rather than a part of the connective, has been disregarded. Tables 3.3 and 3.4 are obviously not exhaustive, but they do include most of the possible logical-semantic connections between propositions. The word or words in upper

Table 3.3   Types and Examples of Underlying Propositional Connectives[a]

Type	Examples
Logical conditional (IF/THEN)	(i) If "X implies Y" is true and "X" is true, + then "Y" is true.
Logical consequence (SINCE/ HENCE, FOR EXAMPLE, IN GENERAL)	(i) Since "X implies Y" is true and "X" is true, + hence "Y" is true.
	(ii) All men are mortal, + therefore this man is mortal.
Semantic conditional (IF/P.THEN, P.IF/THEN)	(i) If history were a science, + then in history the causal laws would be more important than the particular facts.
Semantic concessive conditional (EVEN IF/STILL P.THEN)	(i) Even if he wins the nomination, + he will not win the election.
Semantic consequence (SINCE/ P.HENCE)	(i) Another aide pushed aside glistening surface fat + so that vital parts were laid bare.
Semantic concessive consequence (ALTHOUGH/P.NEVER-THELESS)	(i) Although he won the nomination, + he did not win the election.
Semantic temporal sequence or identity (AND, NOW, AND THEN)	(i) The plane took off. + Then I glanced out the window.
Similarity (AS)	(i) He was a blacksmith, + just as his father before him.
Conjunctive (AND)	(i) His name was Anthony. + Hers was Cleopatra.
Disjunctive (OR)	(i) Give me liberty + or give me death.
Adversative (BUT)	(i) It is not armed with superior wit or honesty, + but (instead) with superior physical strength.

[a]The abbreviation "P." denotes semantic possibility or probability as opposed to logical necessity. A plus sign "+" separates the two clauses corresponding to the two propositions.

Table 3.4 Subtypes and Examples of Underlying Identity Connectives

Subtype	Examples
Verb Phrase Complements	
Factive: epistemic verb phrase complement (THAT)	(i) I doubt + that life on Pluto is possible.
Factive: non-epistemic verb phrase complement (FOR-TO, FROM -'S -ING)	(i) You are not allowed + (for you) to shoot the rapids. (ii) You are prohibited + from (your) shooting the rapids.
Comparative: predicate adjective or adverb phrase complement (THAN, AS)	(i) The female of the species is deadlier + than the male. (ii) The male of the species is not as deadly + as the female.
Criterial: predicate adjective or adverb phrase complement (SO/THAT, FOR-TO)	(i) The tablet was so eroded + that it could not be deciphered.
Verb Phrase Modifiers	
Mediative and Purposive: modifier of means adverbial (BY, THEREBY)	(i) By (means of) walking slowly, + the sherpa conserved his strength. (ii) The sherpa walked slowly, + thereby (by this means) conserving his strength.
Temporal: modifier of time adverbial (e.g., BEFORE, AFTER)	(i) Nero fiddled + (at the time) while Rome burned.
Noun Phrase Complements	
Factive identitive: various complement types (e.g., THAT, FOR-TO, OF -S' -ING)	(i) He lied in order + (for him) to conceal his guilt. (ii) He lied for the sake + (of his) concealing his guilt.
Noun Phrase Modifiers	
Identitive: restrictive or nonrestrictive relative noun phrase modifier (e.g., WHO, WHICH, WHEN, WHERE, WHY).	(i) An academician + who became president + was Woodrow Wilson. (ii) The mushrooms + (that are) behind the log + are poisonous.
Nominalizations	
Same semantic roles as nouns: same connectives as used to complement and modify (e.g., THAT, FOR-TO, -S' -ING, WHO, WHEN, WHAT, HOW)	(i) That the slave fled + went unnoticed. (ii) For the slave to flee + was dangerous. (iii) The slave's fleeing + was dangerous. (iv) + How it will end, no one knows.
Various Complex Combinations of Types	(i) (Despite his being) as old as he was, + he nevertheless could not remember it. (ii) (After his) having eaten from the apple, + he was no longer innocent.

case letters are the particular English language conjunctions, prepositions, and so on, chosen for convenience as the underlying "readings" of the connectives (e.g., OR for disjunction). Observe that these readings are the only adopted for the underlying text; they are not necessarily identical to their surface forms. For example, an underlying SINCE/HENCE connection might show up in the surface text in any of a variety of wordings (e.g., *Since* P1, *hence* P2; *Since* P1, P2; P1, *hence* P2; P1, *therefore* P2; P1, *thus* P2; or even simply P1. P2). This is merely surface variation, disregarded in the underlying structure. The possibilities for two successive propositions are that they are either conjoined or subjoined in surface text, or else separated by a period, colon, semicolon, or dash. The same propositions sometimes allow all three surface ordinations. For example:

Conjunction:	*He served as vice-president and then succeeded to the presidency.*
Subjunction:	*After serving as vice-president, he succeeded to the presidency.*
Separation:	*He served as vice-president. Then he succeeded to the presidency.*

Despite the surface variation, the underlying semantic connection between the two propositions is very similar in all three constructions. It could be called temporal succession in the conjunction and separation cases and, for reasons to be discussed shortly, temporal identity in the subjunction case.

The first of these two classification, Table 3.3, is largely self-explanatory. The types that inherently involve succession, namely *Conditional, Consequence,* and *Sequence,* are differentiated by whether the succession is logically necessary or semantically possible (or probable).[2] The remaining types, namely *Similarity, Conjunctive, Disjunctive, Adversative,* and what will be called *Identity,* do not involve the notion of logical-semantic succession. (Perhaps the only distinction in this table that might be criticized as being too subtle is that between ALTHOUGH/NEVERTHELESS and BUT. The latter is used here in the sense of *but instead;* that is, it is used to join two propositions that are identical save for the contrasted elements. Otherwise the former is used.) In some other respects the classification is obviously less elaborate than would have been possible. However, Table 3.3 is grossly incomplete. It treats only the connections between two syntactically coordinate sentences or clauses. Those whose surface syntax exhibits subordination, it is claimed, can all be regarded as identity connections, to be dealt with next.

Table 3.4 presents the same information for these so-called identity connections, namely their subclassification and examples. There are five main subclasses: complements and modifiers of verb phrases and of noun phrases, plus nominalizations. From the standpoint of syntax these are familiar; for example, in a systemic grammar they are classified into "downgradings" and "rank shifts."

---

[2] For the purpose here, the distinction between the semantically possible and the semantically probable (van Dijk, 1973) is left unformalized.

Of course, the present purpose is not syntactic. To reiterate, the rationale for the detailed typology and extensive examples is to cope with the great variety of surface constructions that are encountered. Beside aiding in inferring the underlying connective, Table 3.4 is also intended to support the perhaps fairly obvious point that syntactic complementization, modification, and nominalization all perform the same logical-semantic function, namely the specification of identity. Examination of a few of the subtypes supports this claim. The role of the complement of an epistemic verb such as *know, believe, doubt, hope,* or *say* is to identify the particular fact known, belief held, and so on. Likewise, the role of the comparative subclause is to identify the standard against which the comparison is being made. As to the verb phrase modifiers, they function to identify the time or means (and so on) being referred to. Noun phrase modifiers and complements fulfill similar roles. Nominalizations identify any semantic case slot entries that have been derived from entire propositions.

What remains is to summarize the application to the four brief passages. Table 3.5 shows one measure of the frequencies and propositions of all connective types. Again, the measure is for underlying structure regardless of whether or not any wording of the connective happens to appear in the surface text. Before turning to the conclusions from the table, it is necessary to explain how the frequency measure was calculated. It would not be appropriate simply to count connective frequencies in the underlying structure; such a tally would weight all occurrences equally, regardless of the connective's position in the entire proposition hierarchy (Chapter 4.1) of the text. What is sought instead is a measure that reflects the textual importance of the connective. The connective should be assigned a high score if it occurs frequently or joins major subtrees of the hierarchy, or both. One suitable statistic by these criteria, and the one adopted here, is that each connective occurrence be weighted by the number of propositions it dominates in the text hierarchy. An example taking a subgraph from *State* will illustrate the computation:

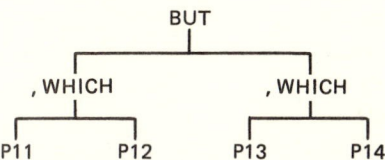

In this example the single occurrence of BUT dominates four propositions, and hence contributes four to the paragraph's total measure of adversative connectives. Similarly, each of the two occurrences of the nonrestrictive form of WHICH contributes two to the tally for the relative modifier subtype of identity connectives.

The weighted frequency values in Table 3.5 confirm the contention that a surface text typically presents a bewildering variety of infrequently occurring connectives instead of a small number of frequently repeated ones. When seeking

Table 3.5 A Statistical Measure of Propositional Connectives in the Four Passages' Underlying Structures[a]

Connective Type	State		Lunchroom		History		Operation		Total	
	N	p	N	p	N	p	N	p	N	p
Logical conditional (IF/THEN)	0	.00	0	.00	0	.00	0	.00	0	.00
Logical consequence: Total	0	.00	42	.20*	123	.28*	0	.00	165	.16
modus ponens, etc. (SINCE/HENCE)	0	.00	42	.20	83	.19	0	.00	125	.12
instantiation, generalization (FOR EXAMPLE, IN GENERAL)	0	.00	0	.00	40	.09	0	.00	40	.04
Semantic conditional (IF/P.THEN; P.IF/THEN)	0	.00	0	.00	0	.00	5	.02	5	.01
Semantic concessive conditional (EVEN IF/STILL P.THEN)	0	.00	0	.00	24	.06	0	.00	24	.02
Semantic consequence (SINCE/P.HENCE, P.SINCE/HENCE)	33	.36*	21	.10	56	.13	119	.41*	229	.23*
Semantic concessive consequence (ALTHOUGH/ P.NEVERTHELESS	13	.14	0	.00	0	.00	0	.00	13	.01
Semantic temporal sequence or identity (AND NOW, AND THEN)	0	.00	105	.50*	15	.03	61	.22	181	.18
Similarity (AS)	2	.02	0	.00	0	.00	0	.00	2	.00
Conjunctive (AND)	6	.07	4	.02	18	.04	18	.06	46	.04
Disjunctive (OR)	0	.00	0	.00	0	.00	0	.00	0	.00
Adversative (BUT)	12	.13	0	.00	47	.11	10	.04	69	.07
Identity other than temporal: Total	26	.28*	39	.18	151	.35*	70	.25*	286	.28*
epistemic complement (e.g., THAT)	12	.13	0	.00	67	.16	32	.11	111	.11
epistemic complement (e.g., FOR-TO)	10	.11	0	.00	0	.00	0	.00	10	.01
comparative or criterial complement (e.g., THAN)	0	.00	0	.00	28	.06	2	.01	30	.03
relative modifier (e.g., WHICH)	4	.04	34	.16	36	.08	8	.03	82	.08
nominalization (e.g., FOR-TO)	0	.00	5	.02	20	.05	28	.10	53	.05
Total	92		211		434		283		1020	

[a]Asterisks "*" show the two most frequent types for each passage.

to infer the connectives, this variety must be coped with. The classification aids in doing so by reducing the diverse, infrequent subtypes to a few main types. According to Table 3.5, summed over the sample passages, the most frequent types of connective roles are identity and semantic consequence. A number of other connectives occur either rarely or not at all. Regardless of how representative of texts in general these totals may be, the immediate finding is again the comparison of the four passages. Major differences as to their predominant logical-semantic connections do emerge. *State* is characterized by much semantic consequence and identity. *Lunchroom,* a narrative, predictably exhibits much temporal succession. It also displays a fairly high proportion of logical consequence connections, which might seem strange until one finds (see Chapter 5.2) that in this passage a logical argument is inferred to help identify the individuals in the narrative. *History,* being argumentative, predictably embodies many logical consequence connectives. The passage also contains many identity connections, because they serve to identify which facts and laws are being referred to in expounding the thesis. *Operation,* a narrative, also displays much semantic consequence, which turns out (Chapter 7.2) to be attributable chiefly to a major inference of the outcome of the narrated episode. In sum, then, this classification enables us to develop the descriptions and their comparisons well beyond our informal impression of how a text is connected.

3.4 TEXT SUMMARIES AND ABSTRACTS

These two terms are often used synonymously, though a distinction could easily be drawn. A precis of a text might be called a summary if it is produced solely by deletion (usually of entire propositions, but perhaps sometimes merely of elements).[3] On the other hand, the reduction might be called an abstract if in addition to the deletions there are insertions. Not just any insertion would do, obviously, if one were to reflect the intuitive notion of an abstract. An inserted proposition would have to be an abstraction, thus technically either an inferred consequent or a generalization. Element substitutions also qualify as abstractions if they are of generic terms (e.g., *a car* replacing *a Packard*) or if they are indefinite pro-words (e.g., *someone* replacing *Napoleon*). At any rate, the distinction between a summary and an abstract is convenient for the following discussion.

Both summaries and abstracts clearly depend on the text's structure. Only the abstract is based on implicit propositions. But since such propositions are part of the underlying structure, the structure provides a necessary basis for abstracting. The basis is not sufficient of course; the specific rules for summarizing

---

[3] Occasionally a deletion takes with it an antecedent needed for a pronoun or the like in the nondeleted part. When this occurs the antecedent is simply substituted for the first remaining occurrence of the anaphor.

or abstracting must also be formulated. In general, the particular precis yielded will depend on five factors: the structure of the passage in the first place; whether the information reduction is to be a summary or an abstract; the specific rules executed for yielding the summary or abstract; and both what might be called the "depth" and the "degree" to which the summarizing or abstracting is carried out. One text reduction procedure that seems a fairly natural way of handling these five factors will be illustrated next. It operates on the underlying structure, and hence provides either a summary or an abstract, depending on whether one does or does not elect to include any implicit consequents or generalizations.

The *History* graph (Chapter 6.1) will be used to explain the method. Since the present aim is merely illustrative, for the sake of simplicity the graph will be collapsed to a depth of four. That is, below a depth of four, counting from the most superordinate connective, each multiproposition subtree will be collapsed to a single node, such as the one labelled "P4-P7" in the diagram below:

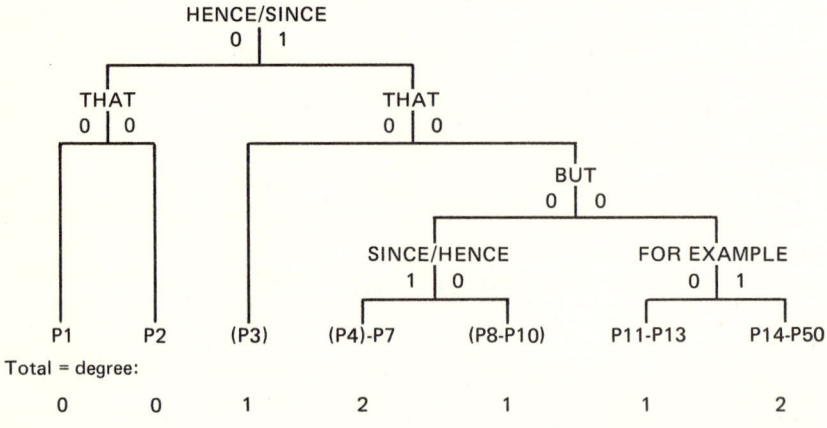

The collapsing does not affect the principles involved (though it does somewhat alter the exact summary obtained), but it allows us to avoid a cumbersome computation for the present illustration.

The crux of the procedure is a single rule based on the connectives: If the connective joins an antecedent to a consequent, the consequent side is considered to be thematic in relation to the antecedent side; otherwise the two sides are considered to be on a par with each other. Only one additional proposal has been found useful for the sample of passages, namely the proposal that with relative clauses the main clause is thematic over the subclause. This second rule is not needed for the present example, however.

Application of this rule, given the tree graph, is virtually mechanical. As shown, each consequent half is assigned a "0," each antecedent half a "1," and each other half a "0." Then, if one makes the probably reasonable assumption that summarizing is commutative (i.e., that $1 + 0 = 0 + 1$ for the integer assignments), one can simply total the numbers in each tree path to arrive at a thematicity index for each terminal node. These totals using a depth of four are given at the bottom of the diagram. The lower a node's total, the more thematic it is. By this procedure the most succinct abstract or summary, the one with degree 0, is just P1-P2: *It can be concluded that history is not a science.* Or to expand on this a bit, one could include the degree 1 propositions. This does not work well for summarization (due to the collapsing of the tree to four levels), because all of P3-P10 would then be excluded. But if one is willing to include implicit propositions, here P3 and P8-P10, the result is: *It can be concluded that history is not a science. (It can be argued that: If history were a science, then in history the causal laws would be more important than the particular facts.) But in history, even if causal laws can be discovered at all, the particular facts still are more important than the laws.* The *If . . .* and *Even if . . .* antecedent clauses remain, but they could be eliminated by going to a depth greater than four. Even for passages less tightly written than *History,* the method seems intuitively satisfactory. The passage whose abstract would be most different from its summary is *Operation.* Its overall consequent theme turns out to be implicit, and hence would be included in an abstract but not in a summary.

Given this procedure, what simple statistical description might allow a revealing comparison of passages? It can be suggested that one indication of a well-composed text is that it is highly stratified; its propositions are distributed over a span of thematicity values ranging from the most encompassing theme to the most incidental detail. Consequently, a summary of a text like this will sharply discriminate theme from detail by including the former but excluding the latter. By contrast, if the majority of propositions are on a par thematically, it necessarily follows that no main theme can readily be isolated. Such a structure is a coherent sequence of equally important propositions. In general, then, a useful statistic is simply the relative frequencies of the various degree values for some chosen depth of summarizing. Except for illustrative purposes, it is reasonable to take a depth large enough that each proposition can be counted individually, instead of simplifying by collapsing into major subtrees as was done above. A quick way of performing the tally is to do it directly on the original, uncollapsed proposition hierarchy. These tally sheets will be omitted here, since they can be easily be reconstructed from the above rules along with the hierarchies to be presented in Chapters 4-7.

The outcome of the calculation for the present four passages is shown in Table 3.6. The tabulation is for explicit propositions only, but the distribution is very similar to what would result from including the implicit propositions. Clear differences among the passages again emerge. *History* approximates the ideal of a wide distribution over levels, permitting a series of progressively more concise summaries. *State* is moderately stratified. But *Lunchroom* and *Operation* are different, one might even say deficient, with respect to their summarizability. Both are diffuse, not pointed. For both the mode of the distribution of themati-

Table 3.6   Distribution of Explicit Propositions over Degree Values

Degree	State		Passage Lunchroom		History		Operation	
	N	p	N	p	N	p	N	p
0	2	.12	11	.38	2	.12	0	.00
1	7	.44	7	.24	2	.12	9	.60
2	3	.19	6	.21	7	.41	3	.20
3	4	.25	3	.10	4	.23	3	.20
4	0	.00	2	.07	2	.12	0	.00
	16		29		17		15	

city values is the lowest value observed, namely 0 for *Lunchroom* and 1 for *Operation*. Hence, for neither would a summary be very succinct, at least not if it were generated by the present method. For *Operation* an abstract instead of a summary would help, because the implicit overall conclusion turns out to contribute three propositions at degree 0. Reflecting on the outcome of this analysis, one would hardly think it coincidental that the two passages with highly differentiated strata are the ones written by well-known authors and intended for serious study. The two relatively unstratified passages are casually written fare intended for lighter reading.

3.5 SUMMARY

The three text analyses introduced in this chapter supplement the main analysis presented in the previous chapter. When applied to a passage each supplementary analysis yields a concisely statable description. In particular, the information analysis calculates the flow of new, old, and contrastive information in a text. The analysis of propositional connectives determines the pattern of logical-semantic relationships among propositions. The procedure for summarizing and abstracting yields a series of such adjuncts, plus an index of a text's summarizability. Among the present sample of passages, each of three analyses reveals nontrivial structural differences.

4. State: A Relatively Simple Argumentative Text with Metaphor and Contrast

4.1 THE STRUCTURE

This paragraph excerpt from Thoreau's so-called "Civil Disobedience" essay was quoted in Chapter 1.1, and statistical overviews of its structure were given in the preceding two chapters. In this chapter the structure and its derivation will be developed. *State,* because of its brevity as measured by number of propositions, as well as its explicitness as measured by the ratio of explicit propositions to total propositions, is well-suited to introducing the layout and notation of the analyses. This also means, however, that we will have to wait until the later passages for significant examples of proposition and element inferences. *State* is far from devoid of interesting structural features, however. This rather powerful, tightly written paragraph is conspicuous for its contrasting affirmative and negative propositions, for its vivid concrete metaphors that vitalize its abstract content, but unfortunately also for a slight obscurity in its overall coherence as a text hierarchy.

The aim of this section is to display the structure derived and to point out its interesting properties. In the next section of this chapter that derivation itself will be discussed. Accordingly, Figure 4.1 presents the inferred underlying text hierarcy, Table 4.1 gives the categorization of the surface text into semantic categories, and Table 4.2 extends the categorization to include the inferred propositions. (For brevity, Table 4.2 has been reduced to an excerpt showing only some of the propositions, not all, in the underlying structure. An informal wording of the others appears later.) More important than the categorization, however, is the fact that Table 4.2 is organized so as to facilitate the subsequent

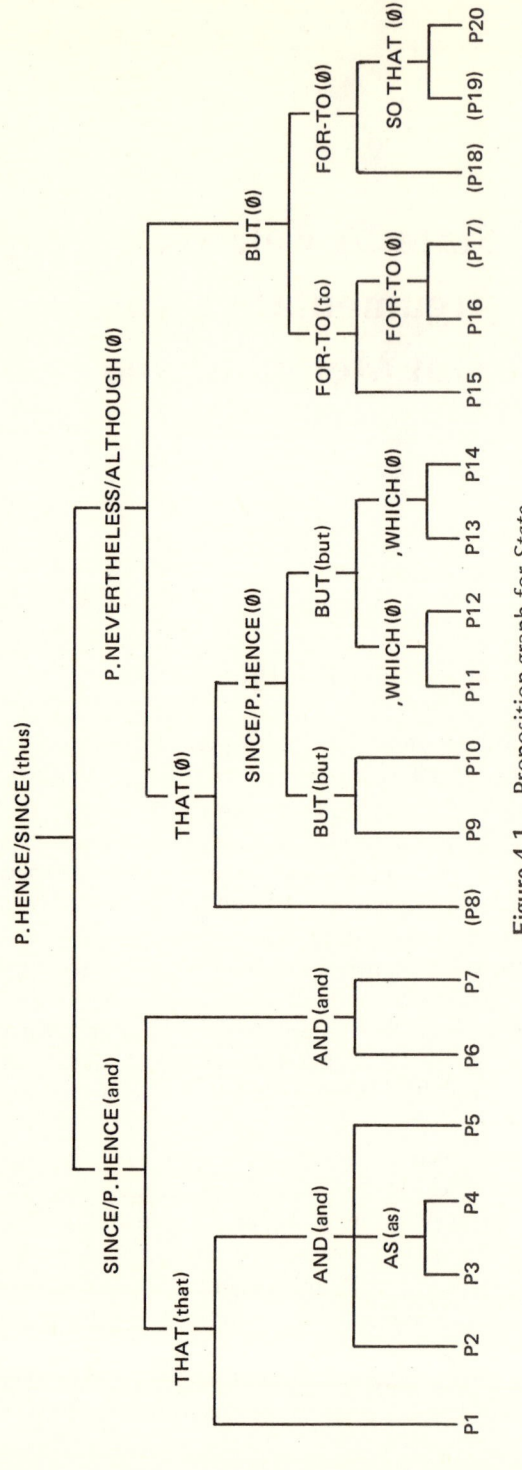

Figure 4.1 Proposition graph for *State*.

Table 4.1 *State* Paragraph, Categorized Surface Structure

Prop. #	Text[a]	Connective	Animate	Action, being	Manner	Inanimate Concrete	Inanimate Abstract
1	I saw		I	had			sight
2	that the state was half-witted,	that	the state	was			half-witted
3	that it was timid	that	it	was			timid
"	as a <lone woman> with her <silver spoons>,	as	a lone woman; her			with silver spoons	
5	and that it did not know <its friends from its foes>,	and that	it; of its friends from its foes	did not have			knowledge
"	and I lost all my <remaining respect> for it,	and	I; my; for it	lost			all remaining respect
6	and pitied it.	and	for it	had			pity
"	Thus	Thus					
7							
(8)							
11	the state never intentionally confronts a man's sense, <intellectual or moral>,		the state; a man's	never confronts	intentionally		sense
"							intellectual or moral
12	but only his body,	but	his	only			body
"	his senses.		his				senses
14							
13							
9	It is not armed with <superior wit or honesty>,		It	is not armed			with superior wit or honesty
"							
"							
10	but with <superior physical strength>.	but					with superior physical strength
"							
15	I was not born		I	was not born			
16	to be forced.	to		be forced			
(17)							
(18)							
(19)							
20	I will breathe after my <own fashion>.		I; my	will breathe	after own fashion		
"							

[a]The symbol "< >" denotes the following unanalyzed constituents: common NP or conjunction thereof in P4 (two), etc. as shown.

Table 4.2 *State* Paragraph, Excerpts from Underlying Structure[a]

Prop. #	Connective	Spatial, temporal	Animate	Action, being	Manner	Inanimate Concrete	Inanimate Abstract
1			(The author)	[had]			[sight]
2	that		the state	was			half-witted
3	that		(the state)	was			timid
4	as		a lone woman; (a lone woman's)	{is}		with silver spoons	{timid}
5 " " "	and that		(the state); of (the state's) friends from (the state's) foes	[did not have]			[knowledge]
6 " "	and		(the author); (the author's); for (the state)	lost			all remaining respect
7 "	and		{the author}; for (the state)	[had]			[pity]
(8)	Thus		*the author*	*had*			*sight*
9 "			(the state); (((to a man's)))	is not armed			with superior wit or honesty
.	.	.	.	.	.	.	.
.	.	.	.	.	.	.	.
.	.	.	.	.	.	.	.
15			(The author)	was not born			
16	to		{the author}	is forced			
(17) "			*the author; the state's*	*breathes*			*after fashion*
(18)			*the author*	*was born*			
(19)			*the author*	*is free*			
20 "			(the author); (the author's)	will breathe	after own fashion		

[a]Notation is defined on p. 51.

discussion of its derivation. Taken together, Figure 4.1 and Table 4.2 constitute the representation of the underlying structure, or to speak more precisely, the underlying text structure, of the passage. It would have been simpler, of course, if the full underlying structure could have been displayed in a single figure or table instead of requiring both. But it turns out that a text's proposition hierarchy best lends itself to graphic representation, whereas the rest of the structure is most clearly conveyed by a table. The first table, Table 4.1 in this case, is simply a convenient preliminary to the second.

Let us begin with the figure which displays the outcome of the derivation, after the propositions, connectives, and their hierarchy have been inferred. Each inserted proposition—that is, each proposition which is either an inference or a parallel—has its number enclosed in parentheses. The only other notation is for the connectives, for example, BUT (*but*). Here the underlying connective is set in upper case letters, following by the surface connective parenthesized and in lower case letters. In this example the two happen to be identical; sometimes the underlying and surface connectives are different, for example SINCE/P.HENCE (*and*). More often the underlying connective is inferred where the surface connective is null, for example THAT ($\emptyset$). Many of the connectives occur in pairs, such as the SINCE/P.HENCE pair. Here the slash symbol "/" separates the two connectives. The intended reading is SINCE left-hand subtree, HENCE right-hand subtree; an example from Figure 4.1 is SINCE P1-P5/P.HENCE P6-P7. When there is only one underlying connective shown at the junction of two subtrees it is to be read as preplaced before the right-hand (left-hand) subtree if it appears without (with) a slash. Thus, P1 and P2 joined by "WHEN" would be read P1 WHEN P2, or joined by "WHEN/-" would be read WHEN P1, P2. Also, the abbreviation "P." in P.HENCE (or P.SINCE) denotes that the consequent (or antecedent) is inferred to be semantically possible or probable, as opposed to a logically necessary consequent, which would be denoted HENCE (or SINCE). Finally, a preplaced comma, for example that in ",WHICH," is used to distinguish a nonrestrictive from a restrictive relative clause.

With the notation in hand, a few observations are in order as to the structure revealed in the figure. First consider the parsing into major subtree or parts of the paragraph. As shown, it has been inferred that the paragraph can be divided into two major halves, a conclusion (P.HENCE side of the connective) P1-P7 and a supporting argument (SINCE side) P8-P20. As stated earlier, a fundamental principle of the theory is that any conclusion or consequent is related to its argument or antecedent as theme: development of theme. Applying this principle to the present paragraph, P1-P7 is identified as the theme and P8-P20 as its development. (Of course, it should be kept in mind that within the larger context of Thoreau's entire essay this local paragraph theme is undoubtedly itself subsumed under some global theme.) Next, according to Figure 4.1, the conclusion recursively divides into its own argument P1-P5 and consequent

P6-P7. Correspondingly, the main development branches into a consequent (NEVERTHELESS connective) side P8-P14 and a concessive (ALTHOUGH connective) side P15-P20. In the next section we will discuss the rationale for this inferred tree structure, mentioning problems with the inference as well as some less satisfactory alternatives.

From the terminal nodes of the figure we can state a heuristically helpful proposition-by-proposition reading of the underlying structure, informally phrased so that the degree of explicitness and syntax of the inferred propositions more or less matches that of the surface text. Casting this reading back again into a paragraph format and using paragraphing to mark the inferred main boundary between subtrees gives:

P1-P7	I saw that the state was half-witted, that it was timid as a lone woman with her silver spoons, and that it did not know its friends from its foes, and I lost all my remaining respect for it, and pitied it.
(P8)	(Because I saw that) it is not armed with superior wit
P9-P14	or honesty, but with superior physical strength. The state never intentionally confronts a man's sense, intellectual or
P15-P16	moral, but only his senses, his body. (Nevertheless) I was
(P17-P19)	not born to be forced (to breathe after the state's fashion).
P20	(I was born to be free so that) I will breathe after my own fashion.

It must be emphasized that this informal version is by no means an actual stage in the analysis. The only reason for including it here is expository, to aid the reader in anticipating and following the technical presentation of the structure in the remainder of this chapter. Nor is any other implication of it intended, least of all the implication that this particular rendition of the passage would be any more or less comprehensible than the original surface text.

Besides the text hierarchy the other aspects of the underlying text are given in Table 4.2, which is accompanied by Table 4.1 as a convenient preliminary. Presentation of these two tables will complete the representation, leaving only its derivation to be discussed. In Table 4.1 the rows indicate the decomposition of the surface text into underlying propositions, which though not syntactically elementary are as close to it as seems practicable for a text level theory. The columns show the within-proposition categorization of text elements into their major semantic categories. The notation is defined as follows: Pointed brackets "$<>$" enclose minor, routine syntactic constituents that for simplicity's sake have been left unanalyzed. The convention is to disregard textually minor phrase and clause segmentations, including determiner + noun phrase, adjective + noun phrase, auxiliary + verb phrase, phrase conjunction, and so forth. Also, blank rows have been left in Table 4.1 so that inferred propositions can be inserted later, in Table 4.2. A semicolon is used to separate any members of the same category in the same proposition. What Table 4.1 adds to the representation is the recognition that this particular text contains essentially only three semantic categories (Chapter 2.3.2) other than the connectives and the two infrequent categories. The three prominent categories are: *Action, being* of course, plus *Animate* and *Inanimate, abstract.* Table 4.1 also highlights the procession of elements within the same category as the text continues; for example, in the *Action, being* column the predominantly alternating pattern of affirmatives contrasted with negatives. Such intracategory relations will be covered later.

Of central importance is Table 4.2, the rest of the underlying structure other than the inferred hierarchy having displayed in Figure 4.1. As stated earlier, Table 4.2 displayed the inferences whose derivation will be the chief issue in the remainder of the discussion. A secondary feature of the table is that it extends the within-proposition categorization to the inferred propositions. It is not so much that the categorization of implicit elements is itself significant, as that the columnar layout of the table aids in quick scanning to spot the referential antecedents; each is in the same column as its respective anaphor.

For these and also future underlying tables, there is notation to be defined. All symbols will be defined now although some will not be needed until later chapters, in which the more complex underlying structures of the other passages are treated.

The symbols (when they occur in a table of underlying structure) are defined as follows:

	Italics.	Inferred proposition (e.g., P8: *The author had sight*).
( )	Single parens around a numeral.	Number of an inferred proposition (e.g., (1)).
( )	Single parens around a noun phrase.	Inferred antecedent of a pronoun (e.g., (*The author*) in P1).
(( ))	Double parens.	Inferred antecedent of a NP, either a reduced, generic, or descriptive NP (Chapter 2.3.1).
((( )))	Triple parens.	Inferred case, verb, or adverb (e.g., in P9 the case entry (((*to a man's*)))).
[ ]	Square brackets.	Regularized element (e.g., [*had*] [*pity*] in P7).
{ }	Curly brackets.	Syntactic recovery of element deleted in the surface sentence (e.g., {*is timid*} in P4).

This notation is very helpful in associating each particular inference in Table 4.2 with the corresponding general rule justifying that inference, to be given in the next table.

4.2 DERIVATION OF THE STRUCTURE

What remains now is to provide the rationale for Fig. 4.1 and Table 4.2, the underlying structure. The derivation is by application of the principles proposed in Chapter 2. Accordingly, the present section is divided into a major part on inferences and a minor part on other derivational operations.

4.2.1 Inferences.

Let us begin with the Fig. 4.1., which exhibits how the propositions are inferred to cohere in a hierarchy. This is the only important respect in which the structure of *State* is somewhat obscure. The interpretation represented in Fig. 4.1 takes as a main conclusion the first subtree, namely that the author saw the state as half-witted, and lost respect for it, and so on. On this view, the rest of the paragraph supplies his reason for this conclusion, namely that although he was not born to be forced (third subtree), nevertheless the state intentionally sought to confront him (second subtree). Conceivably, however, there is an alternative parsing.[4] One might propose that instead the third subtree is the thematic one, the inferred hierarchy being the one diagrammed below:

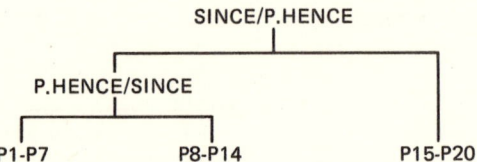

In effect, the state's challenging a man only physically (P8-P14) is seen as the reason for his losing respect for it, and so on (P1-P7), which in turn is his reason for asserting his freedom (P15-P20). But this alternative seems to distort the intended sense of the paragraph. The advantage of original parsing, and the objection to this alternative, is that presumably one would naturally understand P15-P20 as an initial "axiom" about freedom, whose disregard P8-P14 incurs displeasure P1-P7, rather than as a "theorem" whose truth is learned only by hard experience P1-P14 with the state. Of course, in the larger context of the entire essay one would expect this ambiguity to be more readily resolved in one way or the other, though the matter will not be examined here.

One other quite different sort of solution should not be overlooked, though in the present case it does not happen to appear promising. Perhaps in reality the apparent obscurity of the coherence betrays a deeper fault in the

[4]There are other logical possibilities as well, of course. Instead of the figure with the first subtree being thematic, it could be the second subtree, or the third, or any of the three conjunctions of two adjacent subtrees, or even all three (which would be equivalent to none). The only plausible possibility, however, is the one discussed.

analysis, in particular a failure to infer some crucial integrating propositions. For example, the transition from the second subtree to the third might be more compelling if from *The state is armed with superior strength* in the former one infers *The state tries to force me* . . . linked to *I was not born to be forced* in the latter. But this only helps somewhat, and no other major inferences would appear to have been overlooked. Were such inferences to be discovered, the coherence would more properly be described as unclear but clarifiable. This completes the discussion of Figure 4.1.

The rest of the derivation is for the table of underlying structure. The derivational rules applied are tabulated in Table 4.3. The only additional notational symbol is the slash "/," which (when it appears in a derivation table) is used to separate the proposition or element currently being identified from the context pertinent to its identification. For example, "P8/P1" denotes the inserted parallel P8 given the context P1. As another example, under *Relations, intracategory* the entry *sense/wit* records the judgment that *sense* is semantically related to its recent predecessor *wit*. More important than the notation is the overall organization of Table 4.3. It is meant to be read in conjunction with the immediately preceding table (Table 4.2) of underlying structure. For each inference or regularization denoted in the structure table, there is an entry in, or a footnote to, the derivation table. The structure table tells what is inferred, while the derivation table gives the basis for the inference. As an example, in P9 the entry *(the state)* in Table 4.2 corresponds to the entry *Antec. Pro. (it)* in Table 4.3. This denotes the inference of *the state* here as the antecedent of the pronoun *it*. As another example, the italicized row *(8): The author had sight* in the structure table corresponds to the entry "P8/P1" in the derivation table. Table 4.2, the structure table, states the insertion and Table 4.3, the deviation table, gives the rule, in this case regularization in the context of P1. (Recall that, somewhat arbitrarily, parallelism regularization is the one type of insertion of full propositions that is not classified as an inference.)

Beginning with inferences of entire propositions, according to Table 4.3 there are none in *State*. Next in the table, there are numerous inferences of elements of propositions. However, it happens that most of these are quite routine, being merely pronoun antecedents. About the only elements worth mentioning are the pronoun *I* in P1 and elsewhere, whose antecedent is easily understood to be *the author* (Thoreau), plus the semantic case *to a man's* inferred for the predicate *is superior* in P9 and P10. For both of these the antecedent is *a priori* in relation to this one paragraph, though perhaps not in in relation to the whole essay.

4.2.2. Other derivations.

State is the only one of the passages for which these other properties are more interesting than the inferences. Both intracategory relations and metaphors stand out, though a couple of regularizations can also be performed.

Table 4.3 *State* Paragraph, Derivation of Structure[a]

Prop. #	Inferences Prop.	Inferences Element of Prop.	Props.	Regularizations Element of Prop.	Regularizations Order of Props.	Relations Element of Prop.
1		Presup. Antec. Pro. *(1)*		V. nom. *(saw)*		
2						
3		Antec. Pro. *(it)*				*timid/half-witted*
4		Antec. Pro. *(her)*				
5		Antec. Pro. *(it, its,*		V. nom. *(known)*		*knowledge/half-*
,,		*its)*				*witted*
6		Presup. Antec. Pro. *(I, my)*				
,,		Antec. Pro. *(it)*				
7		Antec. Pro. *(it)*		V. nom. *(pitied)/*		*pity/respect*
,,				*respect*		
(8)			P8/P1			
9		Antec. Pro. *(it)*			Perm. (P9-10,	*wit/half-witted*
,,		Presup. Case *(superior)*			P11-14)/	
10		Presup. Case *(superior)*			(P2-4, P5)	*physical strength/*
,,						*wit or honesty*
11						*senses/wit*
12						
13		Antec. Pro. *(his)*			Perm. (P13, P14)/	*senses/sense*
,,					(P11, P12)	
14		Antec. Pro. *(his)*				*body/intellectual or*
,,						*moral*
15		Presup. Antec. Pro. *(I)*				
16						
(17)			P17/P20			
(18)			P18/P15			
(19)			P19/P16			
20		Presup. Antec. Pro. *(I, my)*				

[a]To save space, the figurative expressions have not been included in the table. They are: metaphor in P2, P5, P9, P10, and P20, and simile in P4.

As for details, there are two groups of regularizations, the one inserting P8 and the other P17-P19. The inclusion of P8: *I had sight* is a formality, accomplished by analogical parallel to the explicit P1. It can be written P1:P2-P7:: (P8):P9-P14. In words, the performative P1 for the conclusion is to the conclusion P2-P7 as the inferred performative P8 for the first half of the argument is to that half P9-P14. The other possible regularization P17-P19 is actually not derivable by a complete parallel, so it amounts to taking some liberties with the interpretation of the paragraph. Perhaps it should not have been included at all. However, it does augment the coherence somewhat, and hence might be worth a brief comment. The idea is to insert P17-P19 as a sort of semiparallel to help bridge the gap between P15-P16: *I was not born to be forced* and P20: *I will breathe after my own fashion.* The partial analogy has the form P15-P16:(P17): :(P18-P19):P20, or in words: *I was not born to be forced (to breathe after the state's fashion). (I was born to be free so that) I will breathe after my own fashion.* However, this parallel obviously commits the fallacy of the excluded middle; the denial of a proposition need not imply the assertion of its opposite. In favor of the parallel, P15-P16 alone: *I was born to be forced* does seem a bit wanting in specificity.

Moving to the next column of Table 4.3, there are three regularizations of elements of propositions. These are also of secondary concern. Their only purpose is to transfer all elements referring to mental or moral qualities to a common text category so as to heighten their comparison or contrast. For example, the original *I lost . . . respect for the state and pitied it* can be more consistently, if not more sharply, phrased as *I lost . . . respect for the state and had pity for it.* Similarly, the verb *know* becomes the noun *knowledge* in the context of the nouns *wit, sense,* and the like. A couple of regularizations of the sequence of propositions can also be performed. The one that puts P13 immediately before P14 was mentioned in Chapter 2.3.2. The other permutation places P9-P10 on the asserted state's qualities ahead of P11-P14 on the state's actions. The ordering is perhaps more consistent with the first sentence, wherein P2-P4 on qualities also precedes P5 on implied actions.

Particularly striking in *State* is its contrastive tone, as revealed by the prevalence of intracategory relations among the affirmed and denied abstract qualities. In keeping with this contrastive tone, the relations are primarily cohyponymy (coordination) (for example *honesty/wit*) rather than identity, set inclusion, as so forth. The prominence of coordinate elements invites comparison with *History,* which as we will see is also unmistakably contrastive (as well as abstract and argumentative). But there is a definite difference between the two patterns of intracategory relations. *State* is marked by variety, the marshalling of a series of moral and intellectual contrasts between the individual and the state. To put it succinctly, *State* exhibits a "variation on a theme" development, each contrast being in effect a variation. It will turn out that

History exploits contrast quite differently. There the same contrasts (for example *facts/laws*) tend to be repeated rather than succeeded with related contrasts as the text progresses. Perhaps a reason for the difference is that in *History* the argument is more intellectual and less emotional than in *State.* The emphasis is more on demonstration, less on remonstration.

Finally, and importantly, figurative expressions lend *State* much of its rhetorical force. The motif is the anthropomorphic metaphor of the state as a person, for example, in the phrase *The state was half-witted.* A singular simile is injected at one point for emphasis: *timid as a lone woman with her silver spoons.* Along with the anthropomorphisms there are metaphors that simply replace pale abstract words with vivid concrete ones—for example *breathe* in *I will breathe after my own fashion.*

4.3 SUMMARY

The most notable features of the text structure of *State,* then, are:

1. The passage is predominantly abstract, attributing moral, intellectual, and physical qualities to the state.
2. The passage is argumentative; or, perhaps better, it is exhortative, since the argument is more rephrased than developed. Although first person reference also enters, narration remains undeveloped.
3. The coherence—that is, the coherence of the propositions as a text hierarchy—requires some inferences that are less than obvious. The solution proposed does seem a satisfactory resolution of the ambiguity, however.
4. No inferred propositions at all are found.
5. Inferences of propositional elements, though moderately frequent, are mostly routine.
6. Stylistic variation provides some relief from the tight exposition. Conversely, regularizations were suggested that would make the style more rigid, more meticulously consistent.
7. Intracategory relations, both numerous and diverse, are resourcefully exploited. The effect is a passage with tandem contrasts, namely affirmation-denial on the one hand and diverse coordinate abstract qualities on the other.
8. Figurative expressions are skillfully used to dramatize the abstract argument. Anthropomorphic metaphor is especially powerful.
9. According to the information analysis presented in Chapter 3.2, *State* is comparatively high in both old information and contrastive information.

10. The classification of logical-semantic propositional connectives (Chapter 3.3) indicates comparatively high relative frequencies of the semantic consequence and the identity connections.

11. *State* can be rather concisely summarized (Chapter 3.4).

From this profile one can better appreciate the interplay of the various structural devices. Abstract terms are complemented with powerful metaphors. Unclear propositional coherence is offset by a cohesive fabric of intracategory relations. Stylistic diversity instead of regularity avoids the rigid symmetry that contrasts might otherwise impose. Altogether, a balance of sorts is struck in the exposition—a balance that the theory is capable of discerning.

5. Lunchroom: A Posteriori Referential Inferences in a Loose Narrative Text

5.1 THE STRUCTURE

Lunchroom is a degree or so more complex than *State*, at least with respect to inferences. Both presuppositions and premises are encountered. But in *Lunchroom* their function is still quite limited, being only for reference, not for implication. The passage is self-contained in its inferences; nearly all proposition inferences here are derivable as consequents within the text itself—that is, they are *a posteriori* rather than *a priori*. To mention some of the other interesting properties that will emerge from the analysis, there are: the issue of "cross-hierarchic" connections (cf. Grimes, 1975, pp. 248-255); the inference of a global presupposition for an entire passage; the multiproposition inference of a referential antecedent; the several noncoreferential anaphoric antecedents; and the diversity of intracategory relations.

Figure 5.1 shows the inferred underlying text hierarchy. The table of the categorized surface text, not shown, is derived in the same way as for *State* in the previous chapter. Table 5.1 indicates the categorized underlying text; for brevity only the more interesting portions of the table are shown. As before, this chapter begins by noting the main observations about the structure before going on to discuss how it was derived.

Consider first the inferred hierarchy displayed in Fig. 5.1. As usual, most of it is indeed inferred, as can be seen from the prevalence of null (symbolized by $\emptyset$) surface connectives. To indicate the correspondence between the main subtrees on the one hand and the surface text paragraph indentations on the other, paragraph symbols "¶" have been inserted at the surface boundaries. It turns

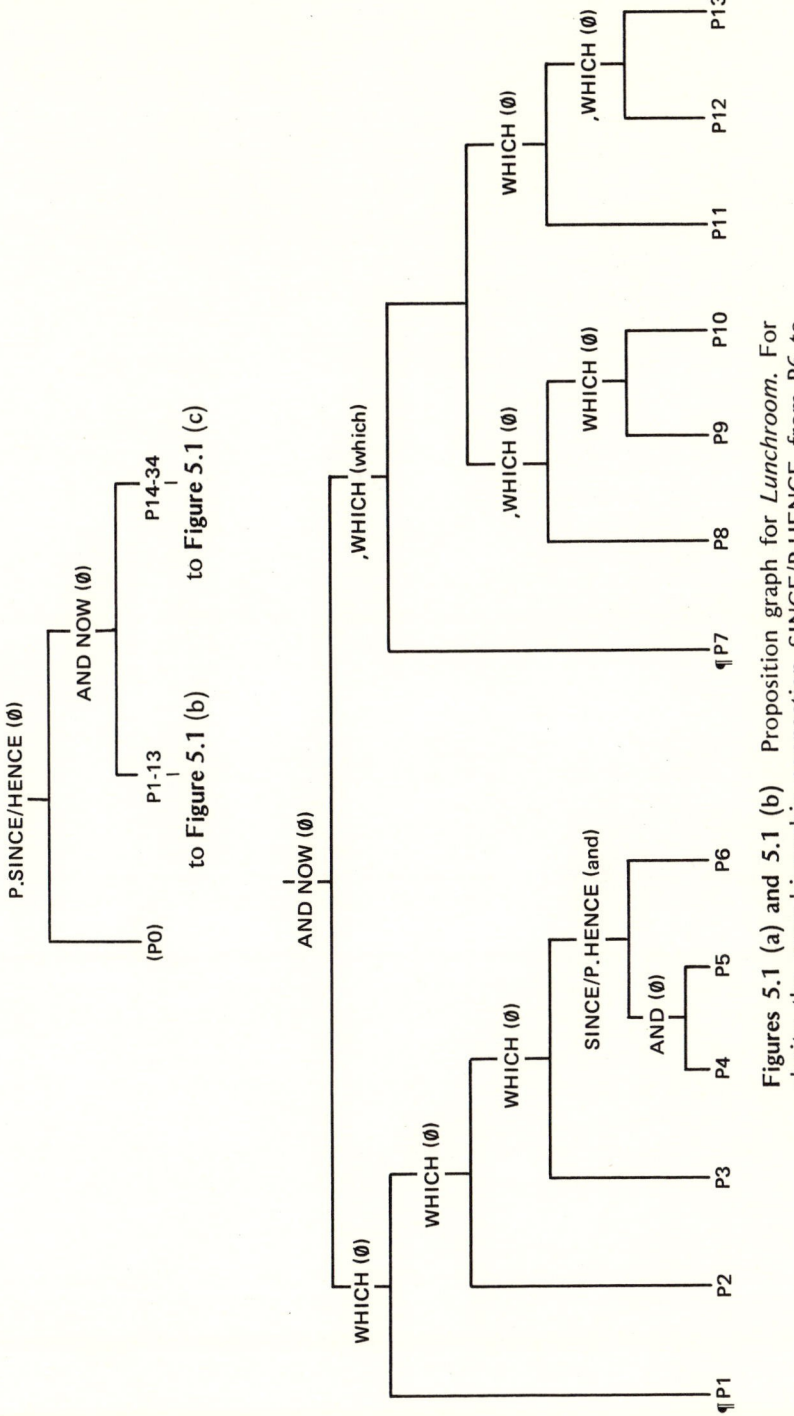

Figures 5.1 (a) and 5.1 (b) Proposition graph for *Lunchroom*. For clarity the cross-hierarchic connection SINCE/P.HENCE from P6 to P14 in the next panel is not shown.

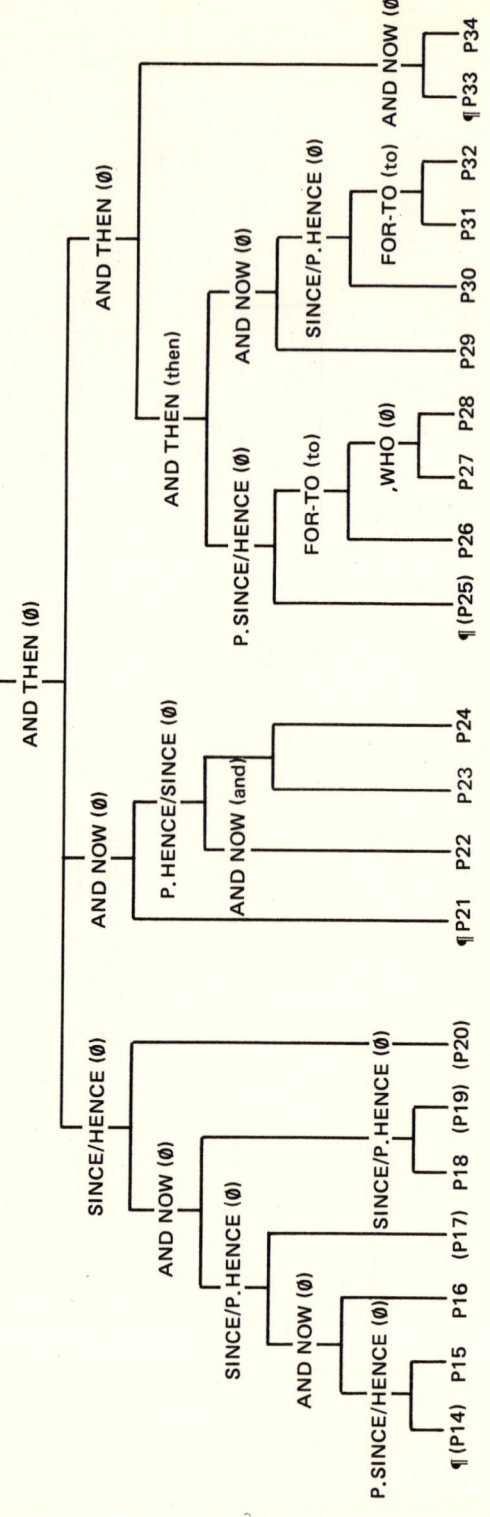

Figure 5.1 (c) Proposition graph for *Lunchroom* (continued). For clarity the cross-hierarchic connection SINCE/P.HENCE from P16 to P25, and likewise that from P20 to P21, is not shown.

Table 5.1 *Lunchroom* Passage, Excerpts from Underlying Structure[a]

Prop. #	Connective	Spatial, temporal	Animate	Action, being	Inanimate Concrete 1	Inanimate Concrete 2	Inanimate Abstract
(0)				began			The event
1		on a summer		began			(The event)
"	.	afternoon					
.	.	.	.	.	.	.	.
.	.	.	.	.	.	.	.
.	.	.	.	.	.	.	.
(14)				was	dusty	A Packard	
15		a few minutes	(((Someone)))	pulled up	dusty	A Packard; by	
"		after one o'clock				the lunchroom	
"						((of the...station	
						and bar))	
"							
16			two men	were		in ((the Packard))	
.	.	.	.	.	.	.	.
.	.	.	.	.	.	.	.
.	.	.	.	.	.	.	.
21			((The other of the two men))	got out		((of the Packard))	
"							
22			(The other...)	felt bad			
23		the night previous	(the other...)	had been		(((liquor)))	
"		((to the		drinking			
"		...afternoon))		heavily			
24	and		(the other...)	bothered	((the intense)) heat		
.	.	.	.	.	.	.	.
.	.	.	.	.	.	.	.
30	Then		(the other...)	went		into the lunchroom	
"						((of the...station	
"						and...bar))	
.	.	.	.	.	.	.	.
.	.	.	.	.	.	.	.
.	.	.	.	.	.	.	.

[a]Notation is defined on p. 51.

out that these do in fact coincide with major subtree boundaries, so the author's indentation agrees with the inferred parsing. Overall, the passage breaks down into an inferred antecedent for the entire passage (see Fig. 5.1 (a)) joined to the major subtree, which is dominated by AND NOW and splits into two halves, namely a two-part subtree (Fig. 5.1 (b)) and a three-part one (Fig. 5.1 (c)).

Figure 5.1 also reveals a couple of oddities of *Lunchroom*, features that would probably detract from its clarity. First, although there is a unifying presupposition P0, the passage has no thematic consequent, either explicit or implicit. Instead, the connectives between major structures are merely the weak temporal ones AND NOW and AND THEN. Also, there are a few connections that might be called "cross-hierarchic," since it is necessary to depart in one way or another from a conventional hierarchic graph in order properly to represent these inferred connections. More about these features later.

The terminal nodes of Figure 5.1 include the implicit propositions, again not in full underlying form but instead in a style more or less congenial with the surface text. It is helpful to see how the passage would read with these included, in order to anticipate what the inferred propositions will be. One phrasing explicit enough for this purpose is:

(P0)	(It began.) It began on a summer afternoon in July, a
P1-P6	month of intense heat, rainless skies, and scorching, dust-laden winds.
P7-P13	At the junction of the Fort Scott and Nevada roads, which cuts Highway 54, the trunk road from Pittsburg to Kansas City, there stands a gas station and lunchroom bar: a shabby wooden structure with one gas pump, run by an elderly widower and his fat blonde daughter.
(P14)	(Since a Packard was dusty, hence) a dusty Packard
P15	pulled up by the lunchroom a few minutes after one o'clock.
P16	(Since) there were two men in the car (hence, the one of the
(P17)	two men or the other of them was the driver). One of them
P18	was asleep. (Hence the one of them was not the driver, and
(P19)	hence, the other of them was the driver.)
P21-P24	The driver got out of the car. He felt bad. He had been drinking heavily the previous night and the heat bothered him.
(P25)	(Since the one was the other's companion) he paused
P26-P32	to look at his sleeping companion, Old Sam. Then shrugging, he went into the lunchroom, leaving Old Sam to snore in the car.
P33-P34	The blonde was leaning over the counter. She smiled at him.

Turning to Table 5.1, it can be seen that unlike *State* the categories *spatial, temporal* and *inanimate, concrete* are now prominent. In fact, within the latter there are two readily distinguishable subcategories, the one for natural phenomena and the other for man-made objects. Note that there is only one manner term, *heavily*, so it is left concatenated with the verb. By inserting the categorized inferred propositions Table 5.1 is completed. Together with Figure 5.1 it represents the inferred underlying structure, whose rationale is discussed next.

5.2 DERIVATION OF THE STRUCTURE

As in the previous chapter, this section is divided into a major part on inferences followed by a minor part on other derivational operations.

5.2.1 Inferences.

Before turning to the inferred propositions, let us consider first the hierarchy displayed in Fig. 5.1. There is an issue worth discussing here, because as in *State* (though not in *History* or *Operation,* it turns out) some ambiguity exists as to exactly what tree structure to infer. The interpretation that seems most cogent is the one shown in Fig. 5.1; it is that P1-P13 (paragraph 1 and 2) provide the background setting for the episode related in P14-P34 (paragraphs 3-6). The background in turn divides into a temporal setting in the first paragraph followed by a spatial setting in the second. The episode itself divides into three subtopics, whose leading explicit lines are *A dusty Packard pulled up . . ., The driver got out of the car,* and *He paused,* respectively. There is an alternative parsing into main subtrees, however.[5] The first paragraph, namely P1-P6, might instead be construed as thematic, with the rest of the passage subjoined to it by the instrumental connective BY. In other words, the sequel would be seen as developing in the first paragraph by narrating how the event began. Otherwise the parsing would remain essentially the same as in Fig. 5.1. Although the matter is not clear-cut, there is an objection to taking the first paragraph as thematic; the first paragraph does not end with P1: *It began . . .* but goes on to add five propositions describing the time when the event began. Yet only *It began,* not the entire first paragraph, is amplified in the subsequent paragraphs. The diagrammed solution reflects exactly this, by presupposing a two-word theme P0: *It began,* to which the first, second, and later paragraphs are connected as temporal, spatial, and temporal (or perhaps manner) developments, respectively. In sum, then, the choice is between taking the first paragraph as the location setting versus taking it as the theme. If the former is chosen, as it has been here, then location setting, time setting, and episode are coordinate expansions on the implicit presupposition P0: *It began.* On the other other hand, if the first paragraph is taken as thematic, then P0 remains as before, only now the sequel is subjoined to P1-P6, developing where and how the thematic event began. But, for the reason suggested, this view seems subtly inferior.

[5] This alternative was originally adopted in Crothers (1975, p. 107).

Most of the remainder of the derivation involves the inferences of propositions and elements. Again, to summarize this information, a table is convenient (see Table 5.2). As anticipated at the outset, there are various properties not encountered previously in the analysis of *State*.

Let us start with the inferred presupposition for the entire passage, namely PO: *It began.* In a sense this presupposition is trivial, especially considering that it is just the main clause of P1-P6: *It began on a summer afternoon in July* . . . . The inference does serve a purpose, however. Without it the main subtrees are weakly connected to each other (see Figure 5.1) by a series of AND NOWS and AND THENS. Some inference, either an antecedent or a consequent, is worth making in order to enhance the coherence. And if it is to augment the coherence of the entire passage, it must then be a global antecedent or consequent for that entire passage, not for just a part. A consequent would be more satisfying, since it would confer some closure on the events. But apparently none suggests itself; that information is the very business of the rest of the novel. Thus, we are left to seek a unifying antecedent, and PO: *It began* comes to mind, because the main explicit subtrees are readily seen as expansions of this global presupposition. That is, not only does *It began on a summer afternoon in July* . . . presuppose *It began,* but so also do *(It began) at the junction* . . . and *(It began when) a dusty Packard pulled up* . . . .

Each of the other five proposition inferences is *a posteriori;* that is, each is derivable from one part of the text and in turn is a presupposition or premise needed for a later part.

First is P14: *A Packard was dusty,* functioning simultaneously as a presupposition of P15: *A dusty Packard pulled up* . . . and as a possible consequent of P6: . . . *dust-laden winds.* If the sample of passages is any indication, this presupposition is unusual in being *a posteriori* rather than *a priori,* thus introducing an interesting matter reflected in the table notation. Such *a posteriori* inferences are written in the order *Presup. & Conseq.* rather than as *Conseq. and Presup.;* this likewise for premises, *Prem. & Conseq.* The ordering reflects a general principle, namely that not until an inference becomes needed as a presupposition or premise is it derived as a consequent of some preceding text propositions. Hence, arbitrary consequents are avoided. Consequently, a glance at Table 5.1 shows that any presupposition or premise bears a slightly lower number than the proposition(s) for which it is needed, and a higher number than the proposition(s), if any, from which it has been inferred.

This same inference P14, and likewise P25 to be discussed shortly, is of theoretical interest in another respect. Each is one of the few inferences encountered in the first four passages that dispute the generally accepted view that a text's propositional structure is strictly hierarchic. (But the fifth passage, in Chapter 8, will be another story). Instead, they are apparently "cross-hierarchic" in character. By this term we mean an inferred connection between only a part of one subtree and part of another. In the present example, P6: *(a month had)*

Table 5.2 *Lunchroom* Passage, Derivation of Structure[a]

Prop. #	Inference	Prop. #	Inference	Prop. #	Inference
(0)	Presup. (P0/P1-P34) &	16	Antec. Def. Gener.	(25)	Presup. (P25/P27) &
,,		,,	NP *(the car)*	,,	Prob. Conseq. (P25/P16)
1	Presup. Antec. Pro. *(It)*	(17)	Prem. (P17/P20) &	26	Antec. Pro. *(He)*
2		,,	Prob. Conseq. (P17/P15 & P16)	27	Antec. Def. Descr.
3		18	Antec. Pro. *(them)*	,,	NP *(his companion)*
4		(19)	Prem. (P19/P20) &	28	
5		,,	Prob. Conseq. (P19/P18)	29	
6		(20)	Presup. (P20/P21) &	30	Antec. Pro. *(he)*; Antec.
7		,,	Conseq. (P20/P17 & P19)	,,	Def. Red. NP *(the*
8		21	Antec. Def. Descr.	,,	*lunchroom)*
9		,,	NP *(the driver)*	31	
10		,,	Antec. Def. Gener.	32	Antec. Def. Gener.
11		,,	NP *(the car)*	,,	NP *(the car)*;
12		22	Antec. Pro. *(He)*	33	Antec. Def. Red. NP *(the*
13	Antec. Pro. *(his)*	23	Antec. Pro. *(He)*;	,,	*blonde)*; Antec. Def.
(14)	Presup. (P14/P15) &	,,	Presup. Case *(drinking)*;	,,	Red. NP *(the counter)*
,,	Poss. Conseq. (P14/P6)	,,	Antec. Def. Red. NP *(the*	34	Antec. Pro. *(she)*;
15	Antec. Def. Red. NP *(the*	,,	*previous night)*	,,	Antec. Pro. *(him)*
,,	*lunchroom)*	24	Antec. Def. Red. NP *(the*		
,,	Presup. Case *(pulled up)*	,,	*heat)*; Antec. Pro. *(him)*		

[a]To save space, only the inferences have been tabled. The other derivations are: 18 intracategory relations (e.g., *month/July* in P3, *gas pump/gas station* in P12, *lunchroom/gas station and lunchroom bar* in P15, and *one of them/two men* in P18).

scorching, dust-laden winds in the first main subtree is seen as a possible antecedent reason for P14: *(A Packard was dusty)* in the third main subtree. If this analysis were represented by a graph arc (omitted from Figure 5.1 because it would have to cross two pages), then it would directly link P6 to P14, thus cutting across the hierarchy. Two possible tactics for preserving a strictly hierarchic graph come to mind. The first is simply to deny the problem by contending that the link in question really should be raised to join the entire two subtrees instead of only P6 and P14. Surely this would hardly do, first because the affected subtrees would then have two different connectives joining them, and, second, because the rest of the subtrees are rather irrelevant to the connection between P6 and P14. The second obvious tactic has more to recommend it. One could simply infer a second copy of P6 inserted immediately before P14. Then P14 would be joined to this copy rather than to the original P6, thereby preserving the hierarchy. The general conclusion, then, is that a cross-hierarchic text is equivalent to a text whose extension by such copying is strictly hierarchic. Both differ from a text that does not require extension to be strictly hierarchic. The choice between a cross-hierarchic graph and a strictly hierarchic extended graph is a matter of taste. The former is illustrated in this chapter and the latter in Chapter 7.2.1.

The next inferences tabled are P17, P19, and P20, which will be discussed together since they jointly serve a single purpose. Here too we have an inference that a reader would ordinarily execute almost automatically, yet whose formalization is not trivial. In the present case, the role of these three inferred propositions is to identify the presupposed antecedent of *The driver* in P21: *The driver got out of the car*. The general principle illustrated is that the identification is made as specific as the text allows. That is, instead of settling for a partial identification of the antecedent by the inference P17: *The one or the other of the two men was the driver*, the identification is pursued to completion by P20: *The other of the two men was the driver*. The formal details of the inference are as follows, as usual phrasing the implicit propositions to read smoothly with the explicit ones:

1. P15-P16: *A dusty Packard pulled up....There were two men in the car* is given explicitly.
2. P17: *The one of the two men or the other was the driver* is derived as a semantic consequent of P15-P16.
3. Next P18: *One of them was asleep* is stated explicitly.
4. P19: *The one of the two men was not the driver* is derived as a probable consequent of P18.
5. P20: *The other of the two men was the driver* is derived by disjunctive syllogism as a logical consequent of P17 and P19.
6. Finally, P20 is, in context, presupposed by the explicit P21: *The driver got out of the car*. Hence, the link back to the explicit text is now closed.

Before we continue to the remaining proposition inferences, this derivation raises a theoretical point that requires comment. The treatment of referential inference might be criticized as being inconsistent, because definite descriptions have been handled differently than other anaphors—definite generic NPs and pronouns, for example. For definite descriptions, but not for the other types, entire propositions have been formally inferred in order to establish the antecedent. Why not insert into the representation the corresponding proposition for, say, the generic NP *the car* in P16: *There were two men in the car?* Trivially, this proposition would be *A dusty Packard is a car,* thus identifying *A dusty Packard* in P15 as the desired antecedent of *the car.* But this example makes it obvious that for such inferences, and likewise for antecedents of definite pronouns, definite NPs, and so forth, the proposition that formalizes the coreferentiality is too trivial to be worth listing. The sample of passages supports the conjecture that only for definite descriptions are such inferences typically sufficiently important to warrant additional propositions. However; if the conjecture proves false it would of course be superseded by the general principle of representing all significant inferences.

The final proposition inference is the other cross-hierarchic one, namely P25: *The one of the two men was the other's companion.* Here too the role of the inference is to establish the antecedent of a definite description, this time *his companion* in P27: *to look at his sleeping companion.* Clearly, the antecedent proposition for the inferred proposition is back in an earlier subtree, namely P16: *There were two men in the car.*

This concludes the proposition inferences for *Lunchroom.* One of them serves as a global presupposition for the entire passage, and every other one functions to establish, either directly or in several steps, certain presupposed referential antecedents.

Again, along with full proposition inferences, there are inferences of elements of otherwise explicit propositions. *Lunchroom* resorts to a variety of more interesting subtypes that did *State.* Referring back to Table 2.3, two *a priori* and four *a posteriori* subtypes are now found. The following remarks illustrate several of the subtypes, beginning with those *a priori:*

An *a priori* presupposed antecedent of a pronoun is *The event* (or, if you will, *The caper)* for the initial pronoun *It* in P1: *It began . . . .*

An *a priori* presupposed semantic case element is *liquor* for the object case slot associated with the verb *drinking* in P23: *He had been drinking heavily the previous night.*

An *a posteriori* referential inference is of *the driver* as the antecedent of *him* in P34. More generally, none of the pronouns here is ambiguous as to its antecedent.

An important type not found in *State* is the antecedent of a definite reduced NP. Recall that for expediency the coreferential and noncoreferential subtypes have been grouped together under this heading. An example of a coreferential anaphor is *the heat,* reduced from the earlier introduced *intense heat* by deleting the prenominal adjective. By contrast, an example of a non-coreferential anaphor is *over the counter,* reduced from *over the counter (of the lunchroom)* by deleting that part of the construction which had been introduced earlier, namely the postnominal modifier *of the lunchroom.* Clearly, the particular noncoreferential semantic relationship happens to be *whole* : *part* in this instance, though elsewhere other relations do occur (e.g., *predecessor* : *successor* relating the anaphor *the previous night* to its antecedent *on a summer afternoon*).

It is interesting to note that a few of these antecedents are rather remote predecessors of their anaphors—for example, *a summer afternoon* in P1 for *the previous night* in P23 and *his fat blonde daughter* in P13 for *the blonde* in P33. Such separation increases the memory burden for comprehension. Also observe that anaphora predictably increases later in the passage, after the characters have been introduced.

For the sake of completeness, it should not go unmentioned that of course by no means all antecedents need be inferred. Some are stated explicitly in the surface text. For example, no entry appears in Table 5.2 to record the fact that *Old Sam* is coreferential with *the one of the two men.* No inference is required because the coreference is stated explicity, in P27-P28: *his sleeping companion, Old Sam* (and, of course, the coreference of *his sleeping companion* and *The one of the two men* has already been established).

5.2.2 Other derivations.

Neither regularization nor figurative speech occurs in *Lunchroom,* so it remains only to mention the intracategory relations. Here too a greater variety is found than in *State.* Hyponyms (e.g., *month/July*) and cohyponyms (e.g., *night/afternoon*) again appear, but now both identities (e.g., *car/car*) and set inclusions (e.g., *blonde/elderly widower and fat blonde daughter; one of them/two men/; road/roads*) occur as well. The direction of the set inclusion is noteworthy. In each instance the textual progression is from set to member-of-set, not the reverse. The effect is analogous to the appearance, first from a distance and then close-up, of an approaching figure. To complete the analogy, one might also expect in texts a return to the whole set as the distinction among its members recedes from center stage.

5.3 SUMMARY

Some of the main points brought out about the structure of *Lunchroom* are these:

1. *Lunchroom* is almost twice as long as *State,* as measured by the number of explicit propositions.

2. *Lunchroom* is interlaced with many temporal connectives, explicit and implicit. Furthermore, being a narrative it naturally contains an abundance of concrete terms.

3. As to its essentially hierarchic tree structure, the passage appears ambiguous at one place. But a resolution of the two-way ambiguity can be offered.

4. There is one inference of a global presupposition. Being a presupposition for the entire passage, it enhances the coherence somewhat.

5. The other five proposition inferences are all ultimately for the purpose of identifying presupposed referential antecedents. These inferences all happen to be *a posteriori;* in other words they are themselves derivable as consequents within the text.

6. Two of these inferences are cross-hierarchic, joining proper subparts of different subtrees.

7. On the other hand, *Lunchroom* contains no propositions inferred as premises for main conclusions. There are indeed a couple of inferences that are premises rather than presuppositions, but they function simply as intermediate steps in deriving another presupposition.

8. A wide variety of propositional element inferences is exhibited. In addition to the more commonplace types there are also antecedents of definite syntactically reduced NPs, definite generic NPs, and definite descriptive NPs.

9. Like the cross-hierarchic phenomenon for presupposed antecedents, many of the anaphors have their antecedents some distance back in the text.

10. A relatively wide variety of intracategory relations, including identity and set inclusion, also occur.

11. *Lunchroom* is comparatively high in new information and low in contrastive information (Chapter 3.2).

12. The most frequent types of logical-semantic connectives are temporal succession, plus logical consequence when the inferred propositions are considered (Chapter 3.3).

13. As to summarizability, *Lunchroom* is relatively serial, rather than deeply hierarchical, in structure. Hence, it resists a concise summary (Chapter 3.4).

From this enumeration one might conjecture some sort of tradeoff principle in text structure. Because *Lunchroom* is simple in some respects, especially in being concrete, it can afford to be more complex in other respects, especially in its anaphoric devices. Also, temporal succession is a relatively transparent organization, but at the expression of summarizability.

6. History: Inferences of Premises to Demonstrate a Stated Conclusion

6.1 THE STRUCTURE

For *Lunchroom,* propositions were inferred in order to identify presupposed referential antecedents but not to supply missing steps in an argument. *History* now offers examples of just another inferences. For one thing, a full causal chain is inferred as a premise for a text sentence that leaps from initial cause to final result. For another, propositions are inferred to explicate exactly how a purported example is indeed an example supporting the generalization. *History* also includes several purely referential inferences of full propositions rather than only propositional elements. In fact, the combined total number of proposition tokens inferred for implication or for reference is almost twice as great as the number of explicit propositions, though this total does include numerous repetitions of the same propositions. Otherwise the structure is straightforward. One possibly unusual inference, a presupposed verb, does occur.

Figure 6.1 displays the inferred hierarchy. Again, the categorized surface text is not shown. Table 6.1 gives a portion of the underlying text structure. In addition, this time a table (Table 6.2) is added displaying the tentative rhetorical categorization, to be discussed later.

According to Figure 6.1 the hierarchy consists of an initial conclusion followed by a supporting argument. The argument has two parts, an assumption of the contrary conclusion and an asserted contradiction of this counterconclusion. Hence, the conclusion follows by standard propositional logic once the

Table 6.1 *History* Paragraph, Excerpts from Underlying Structure[a]

Prop. #	Connective	Animate	Action, being	Concrete	Inanimate Abstract 1	Inanimate Abstract 2
1			can be concluded		It	
2	that		is not			history; a science
(3)			*can be argued*		*It*	
(4)			*are more general*		*the causal laws*	*In a science*
(5)	*than*		*are general*		*the particular facts*	
6			are more important		the causal laws	In a science
7	than		{are important}		the particular facts	
(8)	*If*		*were*			*history; a science*
(9)			*would be important*		*the causal laws*	*in history*
(10)	*than*		*would be important*		*the particular facts*	
.	.	.	.	.	.	.
.	.	.	.	.	.	.
20			was		the reason	
21			{had}		the ((particular))	
,,					fact; {a reason}	
22	that	Napoleon	lost	the Battle of Leipzig		
23	that	(Napoleon)	ate	a peach		
24	after	(((Napoleon)))	(((fought(?))))	the Battle of Dresden		
.	.	.	.	.	.	.
.	.	.	.	.	.	.
31	still		would be more interesting		the ((particular)) fact	[in history]
,,						
(32)≡28		*Napoleon*	*lost*	*the Battle of Leipzig*		
33	than		{would be interesting}		the ((causal)) law	
.	.	.	.	.	.	.
.	.	.	.	.	.	.

[a]Notation is defined on p. 51.

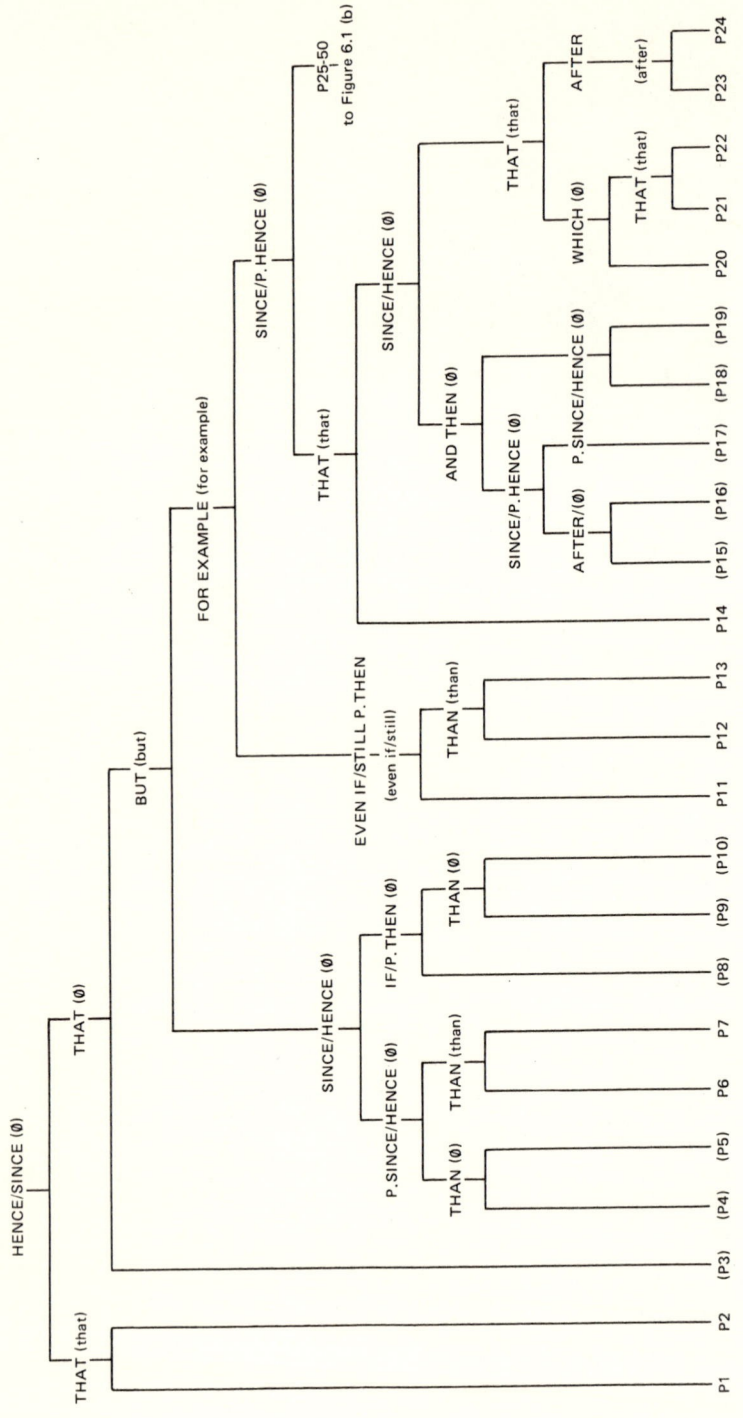

Figure 6.1 (a) Proposition graph for *History*.

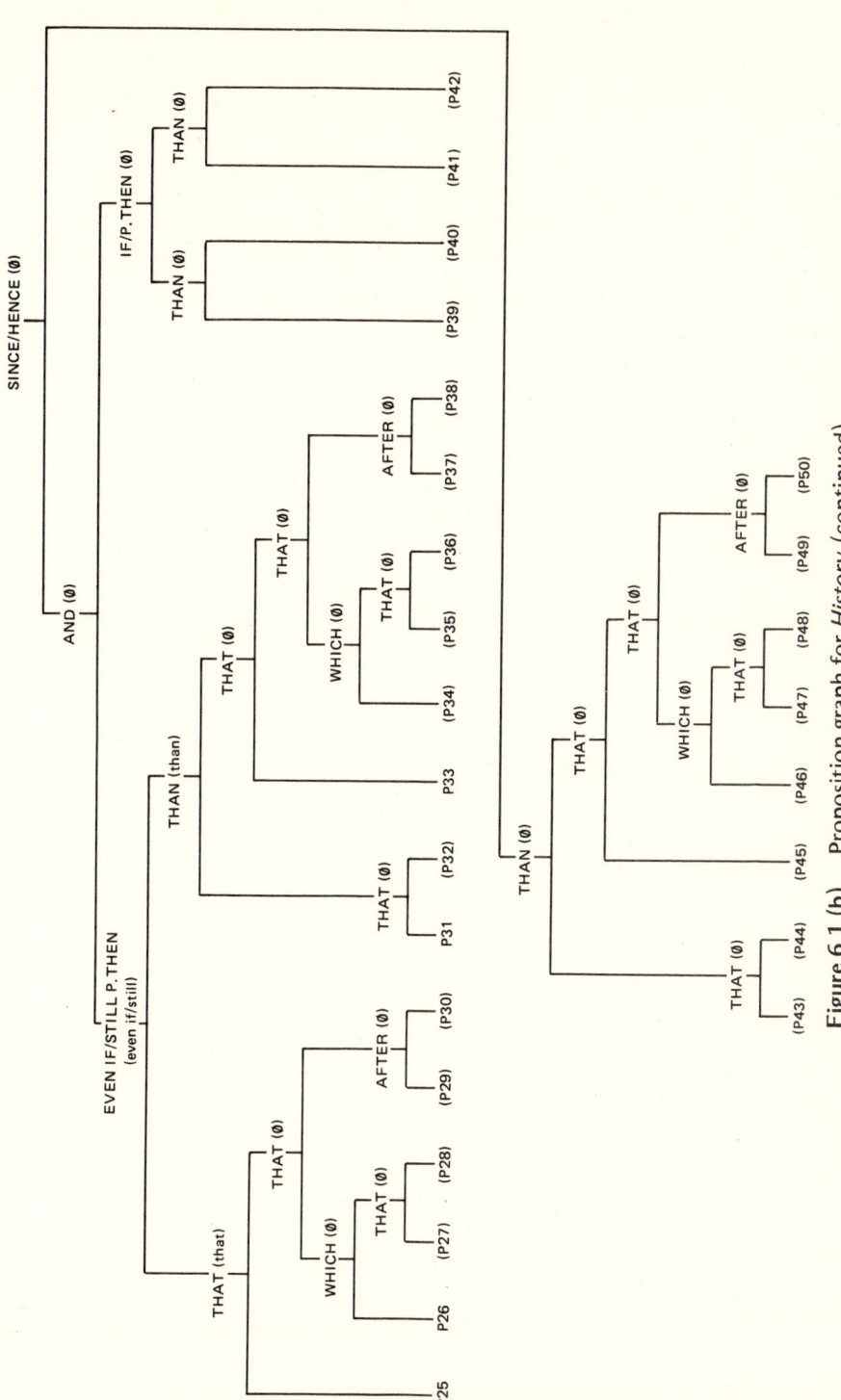

Figure 6.1 (b) Proposition graph for *History* (continued)

Table 6.2 Rhetorical Categorization of *History*

| Prop. # | Connective | Exposition | | (1) Topic and (2) Generalization or Particularization | | Exemplification | | |
		Syntactic Element	Predication	Entity	Predication	Entity	Predication	Entity
1		It	can be concluded					
2	that			(1) history; a science	is not			
"								
(3)								
(4)-(5)								
6				(1) In a science				
"				(2) the causal laws	are more important			
7	than			(2) the particular facts				
"								
(8)-(10)								
11	But			(1) in history				
"	even if			(2) causal laws	can be discovered at all			
12	still			(2) the facts	are more important			
13	than			(2) the laws				
14	For example							
"		it	has been suggested	(1) in history				
(15)-(19)	that							
20				(2) the reason	was			
21				(2) for the fact				
22	that					Napoleon	lost	the Battle of Leipzig
23	that					he	ate	a peach
24	after							the Battle of Dresden
25	Even if	it	is confirmed					
26	that			(2) the reason	was			
(27)-(28)								
(29)-(30)						←	this	→
31	still			(1) historical	would be more			
"				(2) the fact	interesting			
(32)								
33	than			(2) the law				

premises are accepted, and the argument moves directly to an example cited for the very reason of supporting a crucial premise.

Reading from the figure, one way of phrasing the paragraph in order to explicate all of the implicit propositions in a style consistent with the surface text is (again using identations to mark the main divisions within the paragraph):

P1-P2	It can be concluded that history is not a science. (Be-
(P3-P5)	cause it can be argued that in a science, since the causal laws are more general than the particular facts, hence) in a science
P6-P7	the causal laws are more important than the particular facts.
(P8-P10)	(Hence, if history were a science, then in history the causal laws would be more important than the particular facts.)
P11-P13	But in history, even if causal laws can be discovered at all, the particular facts still are more important than the laws.
P14	For example, in history it has been suggested that
(P15-P19)	(since Napoleon became ill after he ate a peach after the Battle of Dresden and then Napoleon lost the Battle of Leipzig after he became ill . . ., hence) the reason for the
P20-P24	fact that Napoleon lost the Battle of Leipzig was that he ate a
P25-P26	peach after the Battle of Dresden. Even if it is confirmed that
(P27-P30)	the reason (for the fact that Napoleon lost the Battle of Leipzig was that he ate a peach after the Battle of Dresden),
P31	the historical fact (that Napoleon lost the Battle of Leipzig)
(P32)	would still be more interesting than the law (that the reason
(P34-P38)	for the fact that Napoleon lost the Battle of Leipzig was that
(P39-P42)	he ate a peach after the Battle of Dresden). (And if an historical fact is more interesting than a law, then that historical fact would be more important than that law.
(P43-P50)	Hence, the historical fact that Napoleon lost the Battle of Leipzig would be more important than the law that the reason for the fact that he lost the Battle of Leipzig was that he ate a peach after the Battle of Dresden.)

Before turning to the derivation of these inferences, we finish the discussion of the structure. Table 6.1 shows the three major semantic categories, one for verbs (e.g., *discovered, ate*) and two for abstract nouns (e.g., *causal laws* and *history,* respectively). There are also three minor categories with one or two instances apiece, including one (e.g., *The Battle of Leipzig*) that seems partly abstract, partly concrete.[6]

Before proceeding to the derivation a comment is in order. Earlier in outlining the general theory (Chapter 2.3.2) it was mentioned that besides the semantic categorization, another representation might be useful, one we will call the rhetorical categorization of a text. No such description was tabled for *State* or

---

[6]Incidentally, the propositions as tabled offer several examples of refraining from a complete syntactic analysis. For example, the pseudo-cleft passive construction *It can be concluded that* . . . is left as such, instead of being transformed to *One can conclude that* . . . .

Lunchroom, because within the present system the formulation of a rhetorical categorization has been only cursorily explored to date. However, now the tentative tabulation for *History,* Table 6.2, will be noted briefly. The heuristic advantage of *History* for this purpose is that, being tightly written, it apparently provides a fairly simple rhetorical pattern. In the future a set of rhetorical categories and rules of category membership will have to be developed for texts generally.

Four rhetorical categories are suggested for *History;* they might be called *Exposition, Topic, Generalization or Particularization,* and *Exemplification.* To save space in Table 6.2 and because of their evidently similar properties, the *Topic* column has been merged with the *Generalization or Particularization* column. Within each major category one could further subcategorize *Entities* and *Predications* if desired. In general, the category labelled *Exposition* includes the performatives (e.g., *say*) and related epistemic actions (e.g., *fear, dream*), but only when they are "meta-discourse" for the entire passage. More will be said on this point later. The category *Topic* specifies the general setting, more or less akin to a spatial or temporal background in some other texts, except that a topic is intrinsically related to comments upon it, whereas a background is accidental. The categories *Generalization* (e.g., for *facts*), and *Particularization* (e.g., for *fact*) refer to the statements about collective and individual entities, respectively. The category *Exemplification* is self-explanatory.

Advantages and disadvantages of this particular representation are fairly obvious. The division into major categories does have a structural rationale; that is, the generalizations and particularizations are syntactic complements of the expositions (*suggested that . . .,* etc.) and in turn the examples are complements of the particularizations (*fact that . . .,* etc.). On the other hand, if a categorization is uncompromisingly rhetorical instead of partly semantic, then an apparently inescapable outcome is that the categorization is semantically incongruous. For instance, *the Battle of Leipzig* and *a peach* are strange bedfellows semantically. By the same token, semantically identical elements get classified separately if their rhetorical roles differ. (To understand this, suppose that the first sentence *It can be concluded that history is not a science* were replaced by *It is a fact that history is not a science.* Now *is a fact* plays the role that *can be concluded* did formerly, namely exposition, despite the occurrence of *fact* elsewhere in the role of a particularization.) Confronted with such anomalies, perhaps the best recourse is to retain both the semantic and the rhetorical categorizations. Additionally, it is better to refrain from attempting a hybrid of the two, because such a hybrid could quickly become unwieldly due to the elaboration of subcategories. It would also tend to confuse the distinction between the two theoretically distinct bases for categorization.

Let us now resume the main analysis.

6.2 DERIVATION OF THE STRUCTURE

As always, the main concern is with inferences, relegating regularizations and other derivations to a few brief remarks.

6.2.1 Inferences.

This time Fig. 6.1 requires no discussion, because neither the inferred connectives nor the inferred tree poses any problem of ambiguity. Hence, we can turn at once to justifying the table of underlying structure. Again the derivational operations are recorded in a table, here Table 6.3 As already observed, the chief issue in *History* is the proposition inferences. Scanning Table 6.3, there are five groups of propositions inferred as premises and four groups as referential antecedents. The former are the more interesting and will be discussed first.

Of the five premise inferences, two are clearly classifiable as *Prem.*, two as *Prem. & Conseq.*, while the fifth requires a more careful analysis. To begin with the clear examples of *Prem.*, they are:

P4-P5: *In a science the causal laws are more general than the particular facts.* This spells out what is presumably the tacit reason for the stated P6-P7: *In a science the causal laws are more important than the particular facts.*

P39-P42: *If an historical fact were more interesting than a law, then that historical fact would be more important than that law.* Obviously this is also taken for granted in the passage, because a particular example with *interesting* as its predicate is alleged to support a generalization whose predicate is not *interesting* but *important.*

The one complex inference actually turns out to be an *a priori* "proof" for what amounts to a familiar *It can be proven that* . . . sort of statement. In the present paragraph, the inference is multipropositional, and its role is to supply a rationale for the otherwise astonishing P20-P24: *The reason Napoleon lost the Battle of Leipzig was that he ate a peach after the Battle of Dresden.* The solution to be proposed has the following form: SINCE first cause led to second cause AND THEN second cause led to result, HENCE by transitivity first cause was the prime cause for result, where:

first cause = *Napoleon ate a peach* . . .
(second cause = *Napoleon became ill)*
result   = *Napoleon lost the Battle of Leipzig.*

The only truly new proposition is the second cause, because the first cause and the result are identical to the stated P23 and P22, respectively. Graphically, the inferred subtree is:

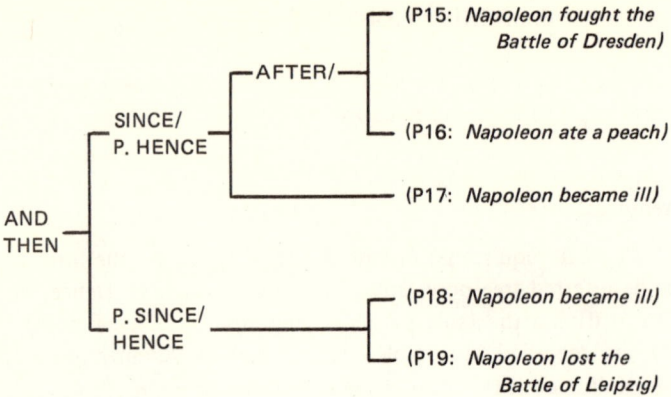

This is joined by SINCE/HENCE to its explicit consequent P20-P24: *The reason for the fact that Napoleon lost the Battle of Leipzig was that he ate a peach after the Battle of Dresden.* In other words, the gist of the analysis is that an expanded causal chain P15-P19 is implicit in its transitive telescoping P20-P24 to only its first and last members. As for the classification of the inference as *Prem.* or instead as *Prem. & Conseq.,* there are two ways of viewing the matter. If one wishes to classify only the propositions not identical to any explicit ones, namely P17-P18, then according to the above graph they are *Prem. & Conseq.* But if one wishes to classify the entire inferred causal chain P15-P19, then it is *Prem.* The latter soution is preferable, because it is the whole chain, not just the new propositions, that has to be inferred in order to supply the desired antecedent for the stated transitive conclusion P20-P24.

The two examples of *Prem. & Conseq.,* by definition, serve to fill gaps between stated premises and conclusions. The first example is P8-P10, obviously a particularization of the stated P6-P7. The second is P43-P50: *The historical fact that Napoleon lost the Battle of Leipzig would be more important than the law that the reason Napoleon lost the Battle of Leipzig was that he ate a peach after the Battle of Dresden.* This serves as an instantiation premise for the inductive generalization about history, namely P11-P13: *In history, . . . the particular facts are more important than the laws.* At the same time the inference is a consequent of P31-P38, which states the particularization for *interesting* instead of *important,* conjoined with the *a priori* premise P39-P42, which takes us from *interesting* to *important.*

Unlike the other passages, *History* also has a few routine examples of referential inferences of entire propositions. Here all such antecedent propositions are introduced earlier in the text, so the *a posteriori* inferences are just repetitions. For example, the inference of P32, identical to the earlier P22, serves to expand the reduced NP *the historical fact* to its original antecedent *the historical fact that Napoleon lost the Battle of Leipzig.*

Element inferences of referential antecedents are likewise routine (e.g., trivial recoveries of deleted modifiers, yielding *the particular facts* and *the*

Table 6.3 *History* Paragraph, Derivation of Structure[a]

Prop. #	Inference	Prop. #	Inference	Prop. #	Inference
1		(17)		31	Antec. Def. Red. NP *(the*
2		(18)≡17		"	*fact)*
(3)		(19)≡22		(32)≡28	Antec. Def. Red. NP *(the*
(4)	Prem. (P4-5/P6-7) &	20		"	*historical fact)*
(5)		21	Antec. Def. Red. NP *(the*	33	Antec. Def. Red. NP *(the*
6		"	*fact)*	"	*law)*
7		22		(34)-(38)	Antec. Def. Red. NP *(the*
(8)	Prem. (P8-10/P1-2) &	23	Antec. Pro. *(he)*	≡26-30	*law)*
(9)	Conseq. (P8-10/P6-7)	24	Presup. Verb *(the Battle*	(39)-(42)	Prem. (P39-42/P43-50) &
(10)		"	*of Dresden)*	"	
11		"	Antec. Case *(fought)*	(43)	Prem. (P43-50/P11-13) &
12		25		(44)≡32	Conseq. (P43-50/P31-38)
13	Antec. Def. Red. NP *(the*	26≡20		(45)	& P39-42)
"	*law)*	(27)≡21	Antec. Def. Red. NP	(46)-(50)	
14		(28)≡22	*(the reason)*	≡34-38	
(15)≡24	Prem. (P15-19/P20-24) &	(29)≡23	Antec. Demon. Pro.		
(16)≡23		(30)≡24	*(this)*		

[a]To save space, only the inferences have been tabled. The other derivations are: a regularization of propositions, P3/P1; a regularization of a propositional element, Adj. prep. *(historical)* in P31; a regularization of the proposition order, Perm. (P26-28, P29-30/P20-24); plus 17 intra-category relations (e.g., *a science/history* in P2, *laws/facts* in P13, and *confirmed/suggested* in P25).

causal laws as the antecedents of *the facts* and *the laws,* respectively).[7] There does occur one infrequent type of referential inference, namely in P24, from the elliptical NP *the Battle of Dresden* to the understood expansion *Napoleon fought* (or *won?*) *the Battle of Dresden.* Two element inferences are embodied here. The one is of *fought* as the presupposed verb, a kind of inference a seldom encountered in this sample of passages. The other is of *Napoleon* as filling the agent case slot. The verb inference is *a priori* but the case inference is *a posteriori, Napoleon* having already been introduced.

6.2.2. Other derivations.

There is one regularization of each of the three subtypes, but these are routine and need not be discussed. One other possible regularization has been disregarded, since it would be only a cumbersome formaility.[8]

The intracategory relations here obviously highlight coordination (e.g., *facts/laws*) interspersed with some identity (e.g., *important/important*). In relation to the number of explicit propositions, such relations are more frequent in *History* than in any other of the first three passages.

6.3 SUMMARY

According to our analysis, the notable features of the text structure of *History* are:

1. Obviously, the passage is predominantly abstract.
2. The argumentative rhetorical mode prevails, as indicated both by the performative verb *concluded* and by the inferred superordinate connective HENCE/SINCE.
3. The overall organization of the paragraph is unambiguous, in that the hierarchic coherence is easily inferred from the surface text.
4. The thematic conclusion is stated explicitly and at the outset.

---

[7]The adaptation from Russell does contain a nagging ambiguity here. The generalization can be understood in any of three ways, namely that in history: (1) all facts are more important than all laws; or more narrowly, (2) all facts are more important than the laws causally connecting those particular facts; or even more narrowly, (3) the causally consequent facts are more important, and so on. Obviously only the narrowest sense (3) is what the example exemplifies.

[8]Specifically, the NP the *causal laws* could theoretically be expanded syntactically as *the laws that certain events are the causes of other events* (or something of the sort) in the context of the subordinate clause construction *the law that the reason . . .,* because *cause* and *reason* are here synonymous. By avoiding this complication, and allowing *causal* to contrast with *particular,* we are treating *causal law* as though it read *general law.* This is fine stylistically, though of course one understands that the nongenerality of the historical causal laws is exactly what diminishes their importance.

5. The prose style is sparing. Unlike *State* or *Lunchroom,* implicit propositions abound. Most of them are immediately inferable however, and indeed many are repetitions of explicit propositions.

6. As would be expected in an argumentative passage, such propositions function as premises for stated conclusions. Both kinds of premises, those *a priori* and those derivable from some preceding part of the paragraph, are found.

7. Intracategory relations are quite frequent. Unlike *State* the procession is a repetition of old elements more than a parade of new ones.

8. Though the adaptation of the passage does contain an ambiguity, it is probably minor insofar as comprehension is concerned. At any rate, the analysis disregards the ambiguity.

9. Compared to the other passages in this small sample, *History* is low in new information and strikingly high in contrastive information (Chapter 3.2).

10. In addition to logical consequents, the paragraph also contains relatively many identity connectives (Chapter 3.3).

11. Being an argumentative paragraph, *History* not surprisingly lends itself to succinct summary, namely the conclusion of the argument (Chapter 3.4).

In all, *History* is tightly written, well organized in terms of summarizability, and leaves unsaid that which can reasonably be inferred.

7. Operation: All Main Types of Inferences in One Allusive Narrative Paragraph

7.1 THE STRUCTURE

The two preceding chapters have exemplified several of the important types of implicational and referential inferences. Now we come to a paragraph that embodies all of these types at once. There are referential antecedents, both *a priori* and *a posteriori*. But above all, there are major proposition inferences—of nothing less than the consequent theme of the entire paragraph, not to mention key linking premises and presuppositions as well.

Figure 7.1 and Table 7.1 together represent the underlying structure, except that again for brevity only a portion of the table is shown. According to Fig. 7.1 the paragraph consists of three segments, namely a two-part explicit antecedent P1-P32 plus an implicit thematic consequent P33-P45. No ambiguities arise as to this segmentation into subtrees. Reading from Table 7.1, one way of phrasing the passage so as to explicate the implicit propositions is as follows:

(P1-P3)	(Chief Resident Jones thought it would not be pointless to begin operating.) (Hence) Chief Resident Jones ad-
P4-P7	justed his face mask while anxiously surveying a pale figure secured to the long gleaming table before him. (And then
(P8-10)	Chief Resident Jones thought it would not be pointless to continue operating.) (Hence) one swift stroke of his small
P11	sharp instrument (and Chief Resident Jones made an opening
(P12)	in the skin of the pale figure), and a thin red line appeared.
P13	Then an eager young assistant carefully extended the opening
P14-P16	as another aide pushed aside glistening surface fat so that vital parts were laid bare.

Table 7.1   *Operation* Paragraph, Excerpts from Underlying Structure[a]

Prop. #	Connective	Animate	Action, being	Manner	Inanimate Concrete	Inanimate Abstract
(1)		C.R.J.	thought			
(2)			would not be			without point
(3)		C.R.J.; on a ...figure	begins operating			
4		C.R.J.; (C.R.J.'s)	adjusted		face mask	
.	.	.	.	.	.	.
.	.		.	.	.	.
.	.					.
11		{C.R.J.}; (C.R.J.'s)	[stroked]	once swiftly	{with} small sharp ((knife))	
"						
(12)		C.R.J.; of the...figure	made		an opening in the skin	
13	and		appeared		a thin red line ((of blood)); (((through the opening)))	
"						
14	Then	an eager young assistant ((of C.R.J.))	extended	carefully	the opening	
"						
"						
15	as	another aide ((of C.R.J.))	pushed aside		(((from the opening))); glistening surface fat	
"						
16	so that		were laid bare		vital parts; (((inside the opening)))	
17		Everyone present	stared	in horror	(((through the opening))); at ugly ((tumor))	
"						
18			{was} too large		{ugly tumor}	
19	for	(((Anyone))); (((from the... figure)))	[removes]		{ugly tumor}	
"						
"						
20	now	(C.R.J.)	knew			
.	.	.	.	.	.	.
.	.		.	.	.	.
.	.	.	.	.	.	.
31≡29			{would be}			[without point]
32≡30	to	(((C.R.J.))); (((on the...figure)))	(((further))) continues (((operating)))			
"						
.	.	.	.	.	.	.
.	.	.	.	.	.	.
.	.	.	.	.	.	.
(44)			did not accomplish			the point
(45)		C.R.J.; on the...figure	operates			

[a]Notation is defined on p. 51.

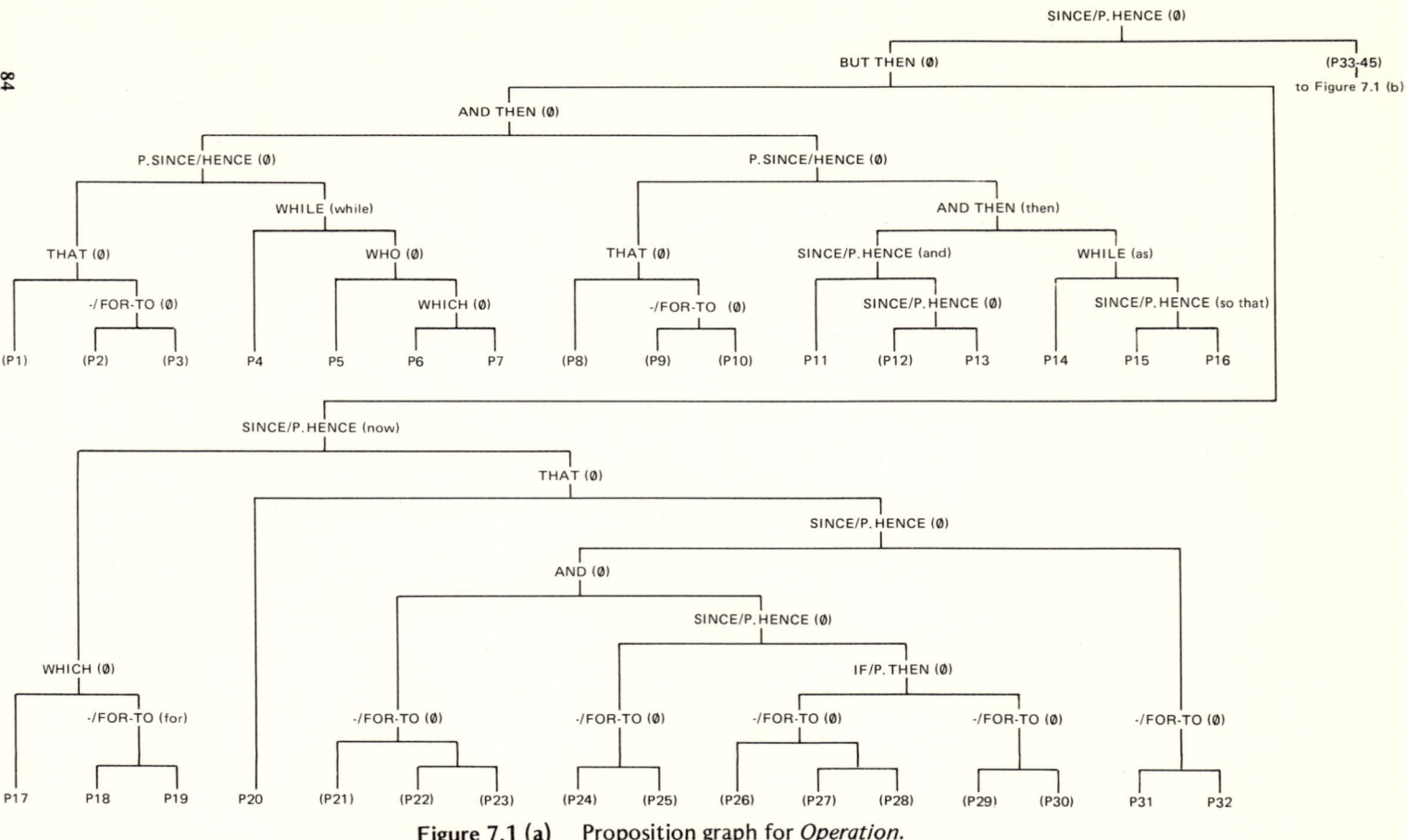

Figure 7.1 (a) Proposition graph for *Operation*.

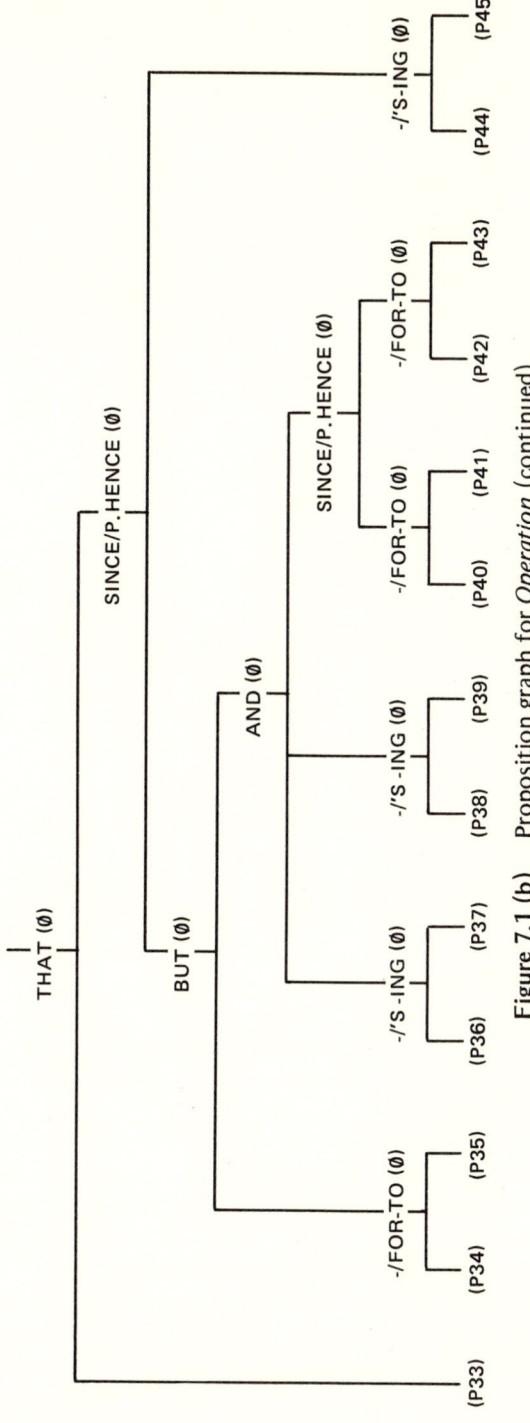

Figure 7.1 (b) Proposition graph for *Operation* (continued)

P17-P19	Everyone present stared in horror at ugly growth too
P20	large for removal. He now knew (that) (because (a) to further
(P21-P23)	continue operating would not be to remove the ugly growth
	and (b1) since the point was to remove any growth, hence
(P24-P25)	(b2) if to continue further would not be to remove the
(P26-P30)	growth, then to continue further would be pointless, there-
P31-32	fore) it was pointless to continue.
(P33)	(Consequently, Chief Resident Jones knew that since
(P34-P35)	(c) the point was to remove any tumor from the figure, but
(P36-P37)	(d1) his beginning to operate did not accomplish the point,
(P38-39)	and (d2) his continuing to operate did not accomplish the
(P40-P41)	point either, and (d3) since it would be pointless to further
(P42-P43)	continue operating, hence to further continue operating
(P44-P45)	would not accomplish the point either, hence his operating
	on the figure did not accomplish the point.)

In passing, note that for clarity the locution employed here is *begin operating, continue operating,* and *further continue operating,* in order to distinguish among the three stages of the operation.

According to Table 7.1 the principal semantic categories in this particular paragraph are *Animate, Action or being, Manner,* and *Inanimate, concrete.*

7.2 DERIVATION OF THE STRUCTURE

7.2.1 Inferences.

To dispose of the inferred connectives first, a few are strong causal connectives that replace weak surface conjunctions, for example SINCE/HENCE replacing *now* at the junction of P17-P19: *Everyone present stared in horror at ugly growth too large for removal* and P20ff.: *He knew . . . it was pointless to continue.* On the other hand, trivial causal connections among presupposed elements are not read into the text; for example, that the reason C.R.J. surveyed anxiously might have been that the figure was pale. Again, the larger the subtrees in question, the more important it is to spell out the details of their coherence.

Of much importance in *Operation* are the proposition inferences. The gist of Table 7.2 is that there are three main groups of such inferences, namely a brief presupposition P12, a series of inferences P21-P30 mediating between a stated antecedent and its stated consequent, and a large group P33-P45 making up the consequent theme of the entire paragraph.

The inference P12: *C.R.J. made an opening in the skin of the pale figure* is simultaneously a presupposition for the definite noun phrase *the opening* in P14 and a semantic consequent of P11: *One swift stroke of his small sharp instrument.* This inference has been inserted immediately before P13 rather than P14, because it also serves as a premise for P13: *a thin red line appeared.*

Table 7.2 *Operation* Paragraph, Derivation of Underlying Structure[a]

Prop. #	Inference	Prop. #	Inference	Prop. #	Inference
(1)	Presup. (P1-P3/	14	Antec. Def. Red. NP	(29)≡31	
(2)	P4-P7) &	"	(assistant)	(30)≡32	
(3)		15	Antec. Def. Red. NP	31	
4	Antec. Pro. (his)	"	(aide)	32	Case, Case, Presup. Verb,
5	Presup. Antec. Def. Red. NP	"	Case (pushed aside)	"	Presup. Adv. (continue)
"	(pale figure)	16	Case (laid bare)	(33)	
6		17	Case (stared)	(34)≡24	Prem. (P34-35/P44-45) &
7	Antec. Pro. (him)	"	Presup. Antec. Gener.	(35)≡25	
(8)	Presup. (P8-P10/	"	NP (growth)	(36)	Prem. (P36-37/P44-45) &
(9)	P11-P16) &	18		(37)	Prob. Conseq. (P36-P37/P1-7)
(10)		19	Case, Presup. Case (remove)	(38)	Prem. (P38-39/P44-45) &
11	Antec. Pro. (his)	20	Antec. Pro. (He)	(39)	Prob. Conseq. (P38-39/P8-16)
"	Presup. Antec. Gener.	(21)-	Prem. (P21-23/P31-32) &	(40)≡31	Prem. (P40-41/P42-43) &
"	NP (instrument)	(23)	Prob. Conseq. (P21-23/P17-19)	(41)≡32	Ident. (P40-41/P31-32)
(12)	Presup. (P12/P14) &	(24)	Prem. (P24-25/P26-30) &	(42)	Prem. (P42-43/P44-45) &
"	Prob. Conseq. (P12/P11)	(25)		(43)	Prob. Conseq. (P42-43/P40-41)
13	Presup. Antec. Def. Red. NP	(26)≡21	Prem. (P26-30/P31-32) &	(44)	&
"	(thin red line)	(27)≡22	Prob. Conseq. (P26-30/P24-25)	(45)	Prob. Conseq. (P44-45/P34-35
"	Case (appeared)	(28)≡23		"	& P36-37 & P38-39 & P42-43)

[a]To save space, only the inferences have been shown. The other derivations are: three regularizations of propositions, namely P1-3/P20, P31-32, also P8-P10/P20, P31-32, and also P33/P20; three regularizations of elements of propositions, namely N. verb. *(stroke)* in P11, Adj. adv. *(swift)* in P11, and N. verb *(removal)* in P19; and four intracategory relations (e.g., *aide/assistant* in P15 and *vital parts/fat* in P16).

The inference group P21-P30 breaks down into a series of steps whose role is to show how the trio P20, P31-P32: *He now knew it was pointless to continue* follows from P17-P19: *Everyone present stared in horror at ugly growth too large for removal.* The details follow (see also Figure 7.1) in four steps, corresponding to the preceding informal phrasing of the underlying text:

At the point labeled (a) in the informal reading, P21-P23: *To further continue operating would not be to remove the ugly growth* is needed as the first main premise for the stated conclusion P31-P32: *it was pointless to continue.* At the same time this P21-P23 is itself a consequent of P17-P19: . . . *ugly growth too large for removal.*[9]

At (b1) in the informal reading, P24-P25: *The point was to remove any growth from the figure* is needed as a formality to serve as a minor premise for the second major premise P26-P30.

At (b2), P26-P30: *If to further continue operating would not be to remove the growth, then to further continue operating would be pointless* is needed as the second major premise for P31-P32. At the same time, this P26-P30 follows from P24-P25.

From P21-P23 conjoined with P26-P30 there follows by *modus ponens* the desired conclusion P31-P32 stated above.

The last group of proposition inferences is P33-P45, the consequent theme of the entire paragraph. Basically, what is inferred is that the operation did not accomplish the point—in other words, was unsuccessful. This is P44-P45, the embedded consequent within the total consequent. But to get to this from the explicit text, the antecedent part P33-P43 of the total inferred consequent mediates. The reasoning (see Figure 7.1) is that what P44-P45 follows from is a one-part premise P34-P35 conjoined with a three part premise P36-P43. In detail:

At (c) in the informal reading, P34-P35: *The point was to remove any growth from the figure* is a duplicate of P24-P25 discussed above and serves as one of the two major premises for P44-P45.

At (d1), P36-P37: *His beginning to operate did not accomplish the point* is the first of the triad that make up the second major premise for P44-P45. This P36-P37 follows from P1-P7, the corresponding explicit propositions about the beginning of the operation.

Similarly, at (d2), P38-P39: *His continuing to operate did not accomplish the point* is the second member of the triad. It follows from the corresponding explicit propositions P8-P16 about the continuation.

Next, at (d3), from P40-P41: *To further continue operating would be pointless* there follows P42-P43: *To further continue operating would not accomplish the point.* Here P40-P41 is simply a copy of P31-P32, itself derived as discussed earlier. Recalling the discussion of *Lunchroom,* the reason for inferring a second copy is merely to avoid a cross-hierarchic link in the graph.

---

[9] Actually, since P17-P19 indicates why the ugly growth was not removable, one could also insert a premise to the effect that the growth could not be shrunken.

Finally, from (c) conjoined with the three parts of (d) there follows the desired conclusion P44-P45: *His operating did not accomplish the point.* That is, (c) identifies the point and (d) establishes that no stage in the operation individually accomplished the point. From this conclusion it follows that the stages collectively did not accomplish it. The formalization of this inference is left unstated.[10]

Significantly, although this derivation is itself correct, it does reveal a rather glaring oversight made earlier in the analysis. What the inferences of P44-P45 correctly does is to end the paragraph with the conclusion that the operation was unsuccessful. But what has been overlooked is that very early in the passage, long before the outcome is known, one already surmises that the paragraph is narrating a medical operation. The inference is both similar to, and different from, the inference in *Lunchroom* of the initial P0: *It began*—similar in that both are presupposed at the very outset of their respective passages, and different in that *began,* but not *operate,* does occur later in its own passage. Exactly how should this presupposition be formalized in the representation? The answer is clear in general but not in particular. What is not obvious is whether a single blanket presupposition must be inferred for the entire paragraph or whether instead we should infer a separate presupposition for each of the three main stages of the operation. That is, the latter solution would read, roughly: *C.R.J. thought it was not pointless to begin operating* as the inferred presuppositional antecedent for the first stage, and similarly for the second. This solution is the one adopted here, and the inference has been numbered P1-P3 in the figure and tables. A possible reason for preferring the three separate presuppositions over the blanket one is that the former will essentially be needed anyway, when the parallels are added. This completes the derivation of proposition inferences for *Operation.*

Inferences of propositional elements are also relatively many and varied in the paragraph. The following remarks single out the most interesting types.

Among the contextually *a priori* antecedents, there is *pale human figure* for the reduced surface NP *pale figure,* and likewise *thin red line of blood* is reduced to *thin red line* in the surface text.[11] Also, the generic NP *instrument* has *knife* or *scalpel* as its inferred antecedent, and likewise *growth* is understood as *tumor* or *cancer* in context. To note an apparently infrequent type, there is a presupposed main verb, namely *operating* for P31-P32: *it was pointless to continue (operating).*

---

[10] Roughly, the formalization would be: *accomplish* in context is equivalent to the union of *accomplish in beginning, accomplish in continuation,* and *accomplish in further continuation.* The simultaneous negation of all three, then, implies the negation of their union.

[11] As with the syntax of explicit sentences, for simplicity the minor implicit constructions have not been fully decomposed. For example, the antecedent has been left in the form *thin red line of blood* instead of analyzing it into NP and postnominal PP. This is also done when the entire proposition is inferred (e.g., *skin of the pale figure* in P12).

The *a posteriori* antecedents include, for example, *aide of C.R.J.* reduced to *aide* in the surface text. There is also one technically ambiguous pronoun, namely *He* in P20: *He now knew . . . .* Here one easily understands the antecedent to be the more remote predecessor *Chief Resident Jones* instead of the more immediate predecessor *another aide.* Another detail is that the indefinite pronoun *Everyone* in P17: *Everyone present stared in horror . . .* has its antecedent *a priori* rather than *a posteriori,* because this antecedent need not be restricted to the three medical people already introduced. (Interestingly, *Everyone present* cannot in this sentence be taken literally, for it does not include the pale figure!)

Minor inferences of semantic cases, especially *a posteriori* ones, also occur. Among the examples are *from the opening* accompanying *pushed aside, inside the opening* for the verb phrase *were laid bare,* and so on, as shown in triple parentheses in Table 7.1. The point of these inferences is that in the surface text the anatomical terms *surface fat, vital parts,* and so forth, are never explicitly associated with *pale figure.* The inferences achieve this association indirectly. For example, given the earlier inference P12 that an opening was made in the skin of the pale figure, the later inferred prepositional phrases such as *inside the opening* then suggest that whatever was inside was probably an organic part of the figure.[12]

7.2.2 Other derivations.

These are both few and routine, so it suffices to note only one here. As remarked earlier, the presupposition P1-P3 that the beginning of a medical operation is being narrated (likewise, P8-P10 for the continuation) or at any rate all of it except the main verb *operate,* can be derived in a second way, namely as a parallel. Specifically, this inference of P1-P3 is parallel to the explicit trio P20, P31-32: on the strength of *He knew it was pointless to (further) continue* one can infer P1-P3: *C.R.J. thought it would not be pointless to begin.* This is similarly true for P8-P10. Even with such parallels the tree graph remains rather asymmetric, however, because a SINCE branch precedes the P20, P31-P32 trio but none precedes P1-P3 nor P8-P10; also, a HENCE branch immediately follows P1-P3 and P8-P10, but not P20, P31-P32.

---

[12] There is an obvious alternative formulation of the inference that can make the connection to the pale figure more direct, but this alternative sacrifices the preposition information. Specifically, the inference could be done via a noncoreferential antecedent (cf. *Lunchroom*) instead of a semantic case, giving, for example, *vital parts (of the pale figure) were laid bare* instead of *vital parts were laid bare (through the opening).* The disadvantage of this alternative is that with *of* throughout replacing *from, inside,* and so on, the specific preposition content is lost. Of course, we could include both kinds of inferences simultaneously—for example, *vital parts (of the pale figure) were laid bare (through the opening)*—but this solution is not greatly different from the one adopted.

7.3 SUMMARY

The gist of the *Operation* structure is as follows:

1. Chiefly, it is concrete rather than abstract (though the main inferred verb *operate* is an abstraction from the specific stages collectively).
2. The explicit part is primarily a narrative, but interspersed are important implicit causal antecedents and consequences of the narrated events.
3. The text hierarchy is unambiguous, having two major explicit subtrees and one implicit.
4. Strikingly, the consequent theme of the passage is never stated explicitly. To spell it out fully requires surprisingly many propositions. This contrasts with *Lunchroom,* in which the overall inference was a simple presupposition instead of an elaborate consequent.
5. Well before the consequence of the operation can be glimpsed, one readily infers a crucial presupposition, or several presuppositions, to the effect that what is being narrated is a medical operation. Like the consequent, this presupposition never appears in the surface text at all. Its representation is fairly, though not entirely, clear.
6. There is also a significant group of inferred intervening propositions, which serve to mediate between a stated antecedent and its stated consequent.
7. Inferences of referential antecedents, both *a priori* and *a posteriori,* are relatively frequent. Semantic case inferences can also be made.
8. Intracategory relations are minimal.
9. The paragraph is notably high in new information, low in old, and lacking in contrastive (Chapter 3.2).
10. The structure contains relatively many semantic consequence and identity connectives (Chapter 3.3).
11. No succinct summary of the paragraph exists, though a terse abstract of it is simply the inferred overall consequent (Chapter 3.4).

The first and third properties might be conjectured to aid comprehension and most of the others predicted to retard it.

8. An Extension and an Appraisal

8.1 INTRODUCTION

This final chapter is devoted primarily to a discussion of the structure of one additional text, namely a revision of the *Circle Island* passage that has been a favorite of past theoretical and experimental text analyses (Dawes, 1966; Frederiksen, 1975a; Thorndyke, 1977). Because text inference is the central component of the present theory, the discussion will be limited to it. First, a reason will be given concerning why the analysis of *Circle Island* is an appropriate closing to this volume. Next will follow an informal examination of that text for the purpose of identifying those interesting properties which an adequate representation should reflect. From these considerations a representation will be sketched, focusing only on the major structural properties that can be identified, rather than on a more complete and detailed description comparable to those developed in the preceding chapters. Following the *Circle Line* analysis, the chapter will conclude with a brief retrospective consideration of the intended linguistic and psychological contribution of the theory. An earlier formulation in the spirit of the present analysis appears in Crothers (1978b).

Why is *Circle Island* appropriate here? Probably the most obvious advantage of this particular passage is that it affords an opportunity for a direct comparison against some other analytic approaches. Through comparison of different analyses of the same text one can form conclusions about the adequacy of the different theoretical approaches for texts in general. Although this comparative aspect will be considered in passing, it is actually only a secondary reason why *Circle Island* was selected here. For the most part the text's interesting properties have not been seriously addressed previously, and hence only limited comparison is possible. Another reason for selecting *Circle Island,* as one might anticipate from the preceding chapters, is to make good the claim that text inference theory can feasibly be applied to passages somewhat longer than the four brief ones already examined.

Yet there is an even more cogent reason for considering *Circle Island* here. Even a cursory analysis reveals that the passage's structure is remarkably complex (which, as will be seen, is not at all the same thing as being merely highly elaborated or detailed). This complexity commends *Circle Island* as ideal for analysis, for it is a fact that nothing is as useful for developing, and later evaluating, a text theory as is an intricately woven text. After all, with a transparent structure a theory is superfluous. By the same token, a text whose structure is only moderately complex will provide only nascent opportunities for revealing instructive differences among alternative theories.

Not only is *Circle Island* structurally complex, but its complexity turns out to be traceable largely to our foremost concern, text inference. Execution of certain inferences, according to general principles for doing so, is a primary means by which representation—either in a reader's mind or in a theorist's description—is accomplished. Hence, the passage is well-suited to assessing the proposed treatment of text inference, and also to extending it beyond the kinds of complexity encountered in the preceding analyses. It is experimentally significant in that it can be seen as eminently appropriate for studies on the role of inference-making in comprehension.

Dawes's (1966) interesting analysis of the passage will not be reviewed here, because it is limited to the set-inclusion relations among the various sets of islanders. Frederiksen's (1975b) theory of text representation is much more comprehensive, a fact reflected in its application to *Circle Island.* One major objective of his approach is the representation of the logical-linguistic relations (implication, equivalence, etc.) that hold between propositions or groups of propositions. Though the general theory is extensively developed, Frederiksen's description of the application to *Circle Island* is quite abbreviated. Only a graph of the relational structure of the paragraph of the island's government is presented. Moreover, his representation in the graph is rather unrestricted; nodes may represent either concepts or propositions, and the relational structure he employs is a general network rather than a specific tree graph. But the internal structure of *Circle Island's* government paragraph, or for that matter any other paragraph of the text, will not be a major issue here. Instead, our focus will be on the more global structure: the relations that exist between larger units such as paragraphs or groups of paragraphs. No mention of these is made in the Frederiksen papers, and thus a detailed comparison with the present approach will not be feasible. A comparison can be stated in general terms, however, for Frederiksen does imply that his graph of the government paragraph illustrates his representation of the entire text. Thus, it is probably fair to infer that the text graph would have basically the same form as the paragraph graph, but with many more nodes and relational arcs. By contrast, we will show that the present approach recognizes some major additional forms of cohesion. Such forms relate the more global units to one another, which results in a very different conception of *Circle Island's* structure. It will be concluded, then, that for text level representation Frederiksen's theory is too weak; it fails to capture the organization of the larger units. On the other hand, his approach is valuable as a treatment of sentence level semantics, a topic not even attempted in the present approach.

Thorndyke's (1977) analysis of the passage is noteworthy on two counts: it deals with the higher units and it constitutes a fairly representative example of the sorts of text grammars that have been conceived to date (Kintsch & van Dijk, 1975; Mandler & Johnson, 1977; Rumelhart, 1975). Therefore, the following observations, though they directly pertain only to the story grammar that has been applied to *Circle Island* (namely, Thornydyke's) are essentially correct for these other current story grammars as well. While Thornydyke does not offer a direct comparison of his method with Frederiksen's, he does correctly note that a story grammar is more a macrolevel analysis. Evidently he means that groups of text propositions are graphed as lower level branches from a macrolevel subtree whose nodes represent such proposed story grammar constituents as "setting," "theme," and "resolution". The passage is thus exhibited as an instance of a canonical form of narrative development. A significant gain in generality is thereby achieved, at least to the extent that the proposed grammar proves to be reasonably adequate. However, the analysis to be sketched here in terms of text inference yields a much deeper representation than does Thorndyke's. This is no accident; the deeper treatment of inferences is precisely what yields the more insightful representation of the macrolevel units. What this conclusion indicates about story grammars is that, though they are extremely promising in principle, the current versions require major additional notions before their descriptive power can suffice to reflect the structural richness found even in so-called "simple" narratives. Analyses such as the one to be given here aid in formulating these notions; some of the structural principles discovered generalize beyond the particular tests analyzed. The outcome of the inference analysis is a story grammar representation of *Circle Island* in particular, but one that also proposes several structure principles for narrative generally and indeed for other literary genres as well.

8.2 CIRCLE ISLAND'S STRUCTURE: PRINCIPLES

Because the main objective here is to focus on the principal properties of *Circle Island,* the narrative was first revised by deleting several inessential details. On the whole, however, the simplification did preserve the original version (Dawes,

1966) both in structure and in content. The revision reads as follows, with sentence numbers added for convenient reference:

CIRCLE ISLAND

1. Circle Island has good soil. *2.* The island has few rivers and hence a shortage of fresh water.

3. The main occupations on the island are farming and cattle ranching. *4.* The farms on the island are affected by the lack of fresh water. *5.* The ranches are less affected by the lack of water. *6.* The ranchers are more prosperous than the farmers. *7.* No ranchers are farmers.

8. The island is run democratically. *9.* Each issue is brought to a vote. *10.* The majority will on each issue is decided by the majority vote. *11.* The actual governing body is a senate, whose job is to carry out the will of the majority. *12.* The senate consists of the richest men, because it is felt that the richest men are the best proven administrators. *13.* All senators are ranchers.

14. The farmers wanted the government to build a canal across the island. *15.* An island scientist had discovered a way of converting salt water to fresh water. *16.* Therefore if a canal were built the farmers could convert sea water brought by the canal into fresh water to use to cultivate the island's central region.

17. The ranchers did not want the government to build a canal across the island. *18.* They did not want the farmers to become able to cultivate the central region. *19.* If a canal were to be built at all, the ranchers opposed a large canal. *20.* A large canal would disturb the island's ecology.

21. The idea of building a canal turned into an issue. *22.* The idea of building a canal was brought to a vote. *23.* All the farmers voted in favor. *24.* The ranchers voted against it. *25.* The vote of the majority was in favor of building a canal.

26. The senate consented to build a canal across the island. *27.* The senate allowed only a small canal to be built. *28.* The canal was so shallow that no water would flow into it. *29.* The canal project was abandoned.

30. Many of the islanders were extremely angry because of the failure of the senate to build a canal that would bring sea water to the central region. *31.* It was likely that there would be a civil war.

Excluding element inferences, which usually serve more to fill out certain details of a text's structure than to clarify the overall structure, the two types of inference proposed earlier are connective (relation) inference and proposition inference. For the purpose of developing a story grammar description of *Circle Island,* it is necessary also to propose a few categories of a text grammar, along with associated rules connecting them. The notions can be quite modest since, it will be recalled, no attempt is being made here to formulate a story grammar itself. Again, although it is convenient to discuss the inferences by resorting to a classification, one should not forget that during actual comprehension or analysis the several kinds of inference-making go on more or less concomitantly. The following organization of inferences will guide the discussion: grammar constitutent identification, since it pertains to the overall structure, will be discussed first. We will see that such identification goes hand-in-hand with certain kinds of relation inference. Next will come remarks on other relation inferences of general interest exhibited in the passage. Finally, a number of observations about the proposition inferences will be made. At this point the observations as to what a representation of *Circle Island* should include will have been completed, laying the groundwork for the actual sketch of the representation.

It is proposed that *Circle Island's* macrostructure consists of five major constituents (of the the form X) and four rules (of the form $X \rightarrow Y$) relating them. Each of these nine terms will now be named and explained briefly:

1. *Generalized Ideal Resolution* (GIR) subsumes the text sentences on the island's governmental procedure for resolving issues in general. As far as the explicit text is concerned, the corresponding sentences are S8-S11.

2. *Generalized Ideal Resolution → Instantiated Ideal Resolution* (GIR → IIR) represents the idea that what the government would ideally do in the instance of the canal issue is a consequent of its ideals for handling issues in general.

3. *Instantiated Ideal Resolution* (IIR), then, is the canal issue instantiation of GIR. It involves how the canal issue should have been handled in order to translate principles into practice. Although IIR is only implicit in the surface text and is quite obvious, including it in the representation does serve a purpose; the discrepancy between it and IAR next is what brings about the climactic conflict of the text.

4. *Instantiated Ideal Resolution → Instantiated Actual Resolution* (IIR → IAR) represents the actual resolution of the canal issue as being, in fact, a consequent of the ideal. The notion of consequence is broadly conceived, as including not only logical, causal, and enabling kinds of consequence but in addition what might be called concessive consequence, in which the consequent follows *despite* the antecedent. The concessive is needed in *Circle Island,* since part of what was actually carried out was the ideal and part was not.

5. *Instantiated Actual Resolution* (IAR) is how the canal issue was actually handled—the principles in practice. In *Circle Island* it is by far the most elaborate of the subtrees, regardless of whether one measures elaboration by the number of explicit statements alone or by the total number of statements including inferences.

6. *Instantiated Actual Resolution → Conflict* (IAR → C) represents the ensuing conflict as resulting directly from the instantiated actual resolution, hence indirectly from the instantiated ideal resolution. What this amounts to is an interesting and not at all unusual nesting phenomenon in narratives: a resolution of one conflict is itself the origin of another conflict.

7. *Conflict* (C) refers here only to the ultimate conflict in the narrative, the islanders' anger. However, the more detailed analysis in the next section will identify additional and lower level conflict subconstituents of some of these five main constituents.

8.   *Conflict → Resolution* (C → R) reflects the text sentence stating that a civil war is probable resolution of the anger.

9.   *Resolution* (R) is the probable higher level resolution, a civil war.

Now consider the evidence for the nine constituents and rules proposed above. Note first that three of them can be taken in pairs, namely the pairs GIR-IIR and IIR-IAR. The two members of a pair differ by a single contrast: generalization-instantiation and idealization-actualization, respectively. Furthermore, for each statement within one member of a pair there is a corresponding individual statement or group of statements, explicit or implicit, within the other member of the pair. Hence, GIR is parallel to IIR, likewise IIR to IAR, and by transitivity GIR to IAR. This parallelism is one of the foremost characteristics of the passage. An example of a parallel is the relationship between the GIR sentence S9: *Each issue is brought to a vote* and the IAR sentence S22: *The idea of building a canal was brought to a vote.* In this example it happens that both of the parallel propositions are explicit. Often, however, one or both of the parallel propositions is left implicit. For example, although the GIR generalization S11: ... *senate, whose job is to carry out the will of the majority* is explicit, its IIR instantiation in the case of the canal issue, phrasable as *The senate's job on the canal issue was to carry out the will of the majority,* is only implicit. Conversely, it can happen that a proposition in the generalization is implicit, while its instantiated counterpart is stated. An example is *On each issue brought to a vote, some islanders vote in favor and other islanders vote against,* obviously corresponding to S23-S24 of the actual instantiation.

Within the present system parallelism is viewed as a significant enhancement of cohesion: The two trees cohere node-to-node in addition to cohering tree-to-tree. It follows that strictly hierarchic representation schemes are not adequate for texts generally; parallelism amounts to a superimposing of node-to-node relations on the tree-to-tree hierarchic graph. It might also be mentioned that in practice the role of any explicit parallels in an analysis is to motivate the original identification of the major constituents, which in turn motivates completion of the parallel by inferring implied parallels.

It is interesting to speculate about possible effects and reasons behind leaving some of the parallels implicit. Perhaps most obvious, an overall parallel between major constituents can be either accented or subdued, depending on the balance between explicit and implicit parallels. (Of course, other text properties including sentence sequence, syntax, and lexical choice also influence the salience of the parallel). Conceivably, what would be optimal for comprehension is that the parallel be highlighted enough that it could be recognized by a reader, but not so much that the text would be tediously stylized. Another speculation can be illustrated with a generalization-instantiation parallel. When the proposition left implicit is one in an instantiation, a reason may be that it is obvious from the generalization, especially in texts such as *Circle Island,* in which the generalization is stated before the instantiation. On the other hand, when a proposition in a generalization is the one left implicit, a reason may be that the generalization alone is trivially obvious. The last example above illustrates this.

Regardless of the correctness of these speculations, however, the central point here is that for *Circle Island* parallelism is a *sine qua non* of the representation. One's comprehension of the generalization-instantiation relationship is crucial to one's understanding of the entire text. Without the generalization the narration of the instantiation, the canal issue, would be unmotivated. Also, one would not understand (or could even misunderstand) the reason that many islanders were angry; here one infers that the anger arose from the relationship between the actualization and the idealization and not from the actualization alone. Of course this discussion does not exhaust the notable parallels within the passage. There are other extensive parallels, such as the one between the farmers and the ranchers. But those parallels are at lower levels of the text rather than between the proposed major constituents.

Beyond *Circle Island,* it is evident that the present treatment is not more than an introduction to the study of parallelism in texts. The purpose here is only to call attention to a major omission in current formal theories of text representation. Hence, the following comments on parallism in general will be brief. The constituents postulated here suggest a few broader categories for texts generally. For example, one might propose a category II *(Instantiated Ideal),* in which subcategories included would be IIC and IIR in the case of narrative texts. Its parallel would be IA *(Instantiated Actual).* Another observation concerns the significance of parallelism for texts generally. It is of course a familiar mode of developing various other rhetorical relationships in addition to those found in *Circle Island.* Among the others are: comparison or contrast, classification-alternative classification, thesis-antithesis, action-counteraction, occurrence-recurrence, actuality-possibility, and actuality-intentionality. Another familiar example is the organization of scientific writing, which often exhibits correspondences between statements of hypotheses, statements of procedures, statements of results, and so on. Other observations pertain to familiar forms of deviation from perfect parallelism. The linear sequence of surface sentences, for example, need not mirror the parallel; there may be inversions. Also, of course, a parallel need not be 1:1, even when implicit nodes are considered. Indeed, *Circle Island's* generalization contains only a single statement about carrying out the will of the majority, whereas the instantiation is expanded into a detailed recounting of what the senate did and what it failed to do. Presumably this is a typical form of text development; narrowing the scope of a discussion goes hand-in-hand with elaborating on the staked-out domain of discourse.

Besides parallelism, a few other matters about inferred relationships between propositions are illustrated in *Circle Island.* Essentially, these involve the fact that some propositions participate simultaneously in nonparallel relationships with two or more other propositions. Two types can be distinguished according to whether or not the particular relation is the same in each instance. For *Circle Island* the matter is simplified in that the number of instances in question is only two, and further in that only a few propositions are dually related to the remaining text. On the other hand, this latter number would presumably be zero for many texts. The possible ways in which an antecedent can be related to two separate postcedents are as presupposition for both, as premise for both, or as presupposition for one and as premise for the other. The first and the third of these cases arise in the *Circle Island* passage.

An example of a statement serving two presupposition roles is S4: *The farms are affected by the lack of fresh water.* On the one hand it is an immediate presupposition for S5: *The ranches are less affected by the lack of water,* and on the other it also leads to a presupposition for S16: *Therefore if a canal were built, the farmers . . . to cultivate the island's central region.* One presupposition of this S16 is that the farmers cannot already cultivate the central region, a presupposition which is itself a consequent of the same S4. (Another way of seeing this would be to infer that the farmers wanted to become able to cultivate the central region. In this case wanting to become able to do something would presuppose that one cannot already do it). Thus, S4 is simultaneously a presupposition for one proposition and a premise of a presupposition for another. In short, its function is essentially presupposition in both instances. Finally, the two instances are indeed separate parts of the text; there is no direct connection between the two presupposing statements S5 and S16. How should this situation be treated in a graph representation of the text? There is little or no reason to favor showing one relationship over the other. Hence, both should be shown. Two alternative methods for doing so will be discussed shortly.

The other situation found in *Circle Island* involves the GIR proposition S11: *. . . a senate, whose job is to carry out the will of the majority.* On the one hand this is a premise for its implied IIR parallel, call it S11′: *. . . a senate, whose job was to carry out the will of the majority in the canal issue.* On the other hand, by introducing the senate, S11 simultaneoulsy serves as a presupposition for S12: *The senate consists of the richest men . . . .* Again, it is necessary to note that the S11 and S12 paths are indeed divergent. The part of IAR to which the S11-S11 path leads most directly is the statement S26: *The senate consented to build a canal across the inland;* this narrates the action the senate took in order to accomplish its job according to the majority vote. Diametrically opposed to this, the part of IAR to which the S11-S12 path leads, via S13: *All senators are ranchers,* is S27: *The senate allowed only a small canal to be built;* this narrates what the senate did in violation of its job. Thus, actually two separate aspects of the government are narrated—they might be called the constitutional (S8-S11) and the habitual (S12-S13). Their respective consequents fan out into two separate parts of the sequel. In short, by virtue of the distinction between the two consequents S26 and S27 we can distinguish between their respective antecedents S11 and S12: S11-S11′ and S11-S12 are separate paths. Which of the two paths is the more important to include in the representation, or should both be included? It can be argued that the S11-S11′ connection is the more important of the two, because S11′ assumes S11, whereas S12 only presupposes S11. Too, a premise-consequent pair is necessarily more cohesive than a presupposition-postcedent pair. Asserting a postcedent requires only that its presupposition be established, while asserting a consequent requires not only this but the establishment of the premise as well. When it comes to representing the connections, then, if graph clarity becomes a consideration one should opt for showing paths such as S11-S11′ in preference to ones such as S11-S12.

Such connections also play a significant role in determining the surface sequence—the linear ordering—of text sentences. Consider the ordering of only the statements being discussed, in particular the explicit ones S11, S12-S13, S26, and S27. Here the adjacencies reflect a *presupposition organization;* S12 and S27 presuppose S11 and S26, respectively. An alternate ordering would be to have premises and their consequents in immediate succession. In this case S26 would be adjacent to S11 and S27 to S12-S13. This could be called a *premise organization.* For a text as a whole, however, the matter is clearly not that simple. In the first place, a description of a text as having one or the other linear organization is decided by the relationships among all of that text's statements, not just the few that comprise a striking example. Examination of all propositions sometimes shows, for instance, that when a statement has two major premises or presuppositions, one occurs immediately prior to the statement in question, while the other occurs much earlier in the text. Also, the discussion here has simplified matters by disregarding degrees of adjacency. We would hardly expect adjacency to be dichotomous, immediate versus remote. Despite these qualifications, we can still say that one linear ordering of a text is relatively more of a presupposition (or premise) organization than is another linear ordering. Taking our example, postponing S12-S13 until directly before its consequent S27 would be—unless there would be other concomitant structural changes—more a premise organization, less a presupposition organization, than that of the quoted text. But necessarily there would be such changes: Moving S12-S13 would diminish its adjacency to its own antecedents, in particular for S13 the antecedent S6: *The ranchers are more prosperous than the farmers* (and in turn its antecedents, etc.) Hence, the postponing could not be done piecemeal. All of IAR would have to be moved as a block, bringing the linear ordering more in line with the representation of the text in its entirety.

We might conjecture that the presupposition form of organization is the predominant one in texts, though of course many texts lack the divergences that render the two organizations distinguishable from each other. The basis for this conjecture is that texts are commonly ordered topically. For example, in *Circle Island* the economy topic in paragraph two is followed by the government topic in paragraph three. Also, a topical organization is a form of presupposition organization; statements that presuppose the same topic are grouped together.

Turning now from connective inference to proposition inference, again *Circle Island* is instructive. One prominent type has parallelism as its textual basis. Recall that after a parallel connection has been inferred on the strength of explicit statements, it is often possible to draw inferences extending the parallel. Hence, the matter might be dubbed one of "length of inference." It has already been noted that, for plausible as opposed to logical inferences, each successive inference of a parallel conclusion stretches the parallel a little more. The inferencing stops with the parallel conclusion to the stated grand conclusion. Though this last parallel may be implausible, it is not impossible. One place where this process leads to interesting inferences that do not connect major contituents (and hence have not already been discussed under that heading) is the parallel between the ranchers and the farmers. What, ultimately, was the farmers' motive for wanting a canal built? Certainly the proximal motive was that they wanted to become able to cultivate the island's central region. (Even this immediate motive is only implicit, however, undoubtedly because it is immediately obvious without resorting to a parallel.) But why did they want this? Pursuit of deeper motives can proceed by identifying parallel statements about the ranchers. Tying together the consequence links for the ranchers, we can see that their being less affected by the lack of water led to their greater prosperity, and in turn to their occupying all the senate seats. It is not totally implausible, therefore, to infer a parallel chain of motives for the farmers, namely that they wanted to become more prosperous and even wanted to hold seats on the senate. Each successive parallel conclusion stretches the inerpretation a little further, but even their wanting to occupy senate seats is not utterly implausible.

This example demonstrates that parallelism is a genuinely distinct type of inference. Inferences of the farmers' possible deeper motives do not depend primarily on one's prior knowledge, as might have been the case had not parallels been stated about the ranchers. Nor do such inferences depend chiefly on any earlier statements about the farmers themselves. Moreover, it is the fact that the motive chain is a parallel, as opposed to being a *consequent premise* (Chapter 2.3.1), that renders the culminating inference implausible. Had the text included a statement for which the farmers' wanting to hold senate seats could qualify as a premise, or for that matter as a presupposition, then imputing that motive would not have been implausible.

Furthermore, *Circle Island* is notable for its sheer number of implications of the types originally recognized in the theory, especially the type *consequent premise*. Some are inferences of single propositions; others (such as IIR, introduced earlier) are of entire major or minor constituents. There are many such inferences. Often, as remarked earlier, an antecedent is "planted." A consequent may not surface until somewhat later, after a second appropriate statement, either a presupposition or a premise, has intervened. A salient example is the statement that the senate allowed only a small canal to be built. While this is an immediate successor to its presupposition that some sort of canal was allowed, it is also a remote successor to its premises that all of the senators were ranchers and that the ranchers did not want a large canal. A second example dovetails with the first. The statement that all of the farmers were ranchers has, as remarked before, one adjacent and one earlier antecedent in the linear ordering.

But neither the sheer number of inferences nor the support for an inference—be it a parallel, an earlier stated antecedent, or whatever—is the most complex aspect of inference in *Circle Island*. Above all, some of the crucial inferences are subtle. To put this another way, certain inferences depend on rather fine distinctions (which is not surprising in a narrative involving competing interest groups and a conflict of interest). The distinctions turn out to be essential to a proper representation of the inferences, for if the distinctions are glossed over then the meaning of the text is distorted, and consequents do not follow from their intended antecedents. Of central significance is the distinction between, on the one hand, a functional canal that would carry water and, on the other, a canal simply as an environmental artefact. The former is implied, and sometimes stated, in the propositions about underlying motives (what the farmers wanted, what the majority will was) and ideals (what should have been built). By contrast, the latter is implied in propositions on actual actions (what was voted on and for, what was built). To reiterate, the rationale for representing this distinction is not the semantic delicacy of the distinction but rather the fact that its repercussions are felt throughout the text. The canal distinction sets up another distinction, namely between those of the island's governmental principles that were carried out and those that were violated. Merely representing the senate as failing to fulfill its duties would overlook this distinction. After all, in the narrative a canal of sorts was built, and both antecedents and consequents of that event figure prominently.

8.3 CIRCLE ISLAND'S STRUCTURE: REPRESENTATION

How might a representation, particularly a graph, reflect the properties of *Circle Island* that have now been noted? Because of the greater length and complexity of this passage compared to those analyzed in preceding chapters, a detailed graph of all explicit and implicit propositions and their interconnections is prohibitively large to be displayed here. Hence, the graph will be greatly simplified and will represent only the properties under discussion. Doing so also supports the original claim (Chapter 1.2) that systematic methods of simplification are feasible. In what follows some of the more elementary aspects of the graphing are developed first. Then, a sketch is given of the representation of the more interesting and complex aspects, namely the major contituents and their parallels plus the major subtle distinctions.

It was observed that S4 functions simultaneously as a presupposition for two different postcedents, S5 and S16. The natural way to graph this is either as in Figure 8.1(a) or (b).

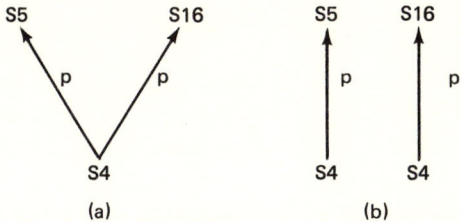

Figure 8.1 Alternative graphs of the divergence from S4. Abbreviation: p. = presupposition.

Figure 8.1(a) depicts S4 as the origin of two separate paths, one leading next to S5 and the other to S16. By contrast, Fig. 8.1(b) avoids divergent paths by the simple tactic of showing two separate tokens of S4, one for each path. In practice, one might perhaps prefer the Figure 8.1(a) solution whenever a graph has few nodes and few divergences; it is the more compact method. However, with more elaborate graphs the Figure 8.1(b) solution proves the more comprehensible. Except for the multiple tokens a tree graph is retained, thereby avoiding nonhierarchic links that detract from the comprehensibility of a graph. At any rate, even this relatively straightforward aspect of the structure cannot be represented by a strictly hierarchic graph. One natural extension or the other is called for.

The other divergence discussed informally was an instance in which an antecedent bore one relationship to one of its postcedents and another relationship to the other. The situation thus differs logically from the one just treated; hence, the representation will differ as well. In particular, S11 was a premise for its parallel instantiation S11' and at the same time was also a presupposition for S12. Figure 8.2 depicts a representation retaining the simplicity of a tree graph, though at the cost of deleting the S11-S12 connection altogether. There remain two separate subgroups rather than two paths diverging from a common origin, S11. The alternatives resemble those in Figure 8.1, but now only the counterpart of Figure 8.1(b) is shown. Since it has been argued that a premise link is more cohesive than a presupposition link, the Figure 8.1(a) type of solution is less attractive here. Another consideration when undertaking a more detailed representation in this situation is graph simplicity. On this basis the Figure 8.2 method is again preferred. Judging from *Circle Island,* for a text as a whole not much information is lost by deleting presupposition arcs such as the S11-S12 one. Few presuppositions are involved in divergences, and those that are

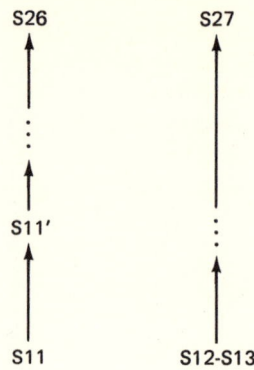

Figure 8.2 Graph of the divergence from S11, not showing the S11-S12 connection.

not are of course retained in the representation. Unlike Figure 8.1, the Figure 8.2 solution preserves a tree graph. (When the remaining text is included, the separate subgraphs will be integrated into a single graph.) However, now the graph is very different *vis-a-vis* the linear sentence order. Any fairly direct mapping of that sequence into the graph has been sacrificed. Now one has to skip around the graph, from one subtree to another and back again, in order to locate the sentence nodes in numerical succession. For texts in general, a proposition that exists any place in the linear order can have a premise at any other place in the order. Hence, the need for a simple mapping, such as bottom-to-top and left-to-right from the graph to the linear order, no longer necessarily exists. Abstractly, this difference in the representation would appear to be rather fundamental.

As for partially implicit parallels, such as the one between the farmers and the ranchers, the representation is straightforward. Recall that the parallel includes both comparison and affirmation-negation contrast, and the concepts being compared or contrasted include the farmers' and ranchers' needs for water, effects of lack of water, productivity, prosperity, acknowledged administrative ability, and, finally, senate membership. The obvious way of representing this is merely to graph a subtree for the ranchers, then to juxtapose the parallel subtree for the farmers. Some suitable notation would be introduced to identify parallel subtrees. Implicit nodes in either subtree would be indicated as such. Together, the notations represent parallelism as being the support for the inference. Each parallel pair of subtrees is represented in this fashion. Actually, there are two parallel pairs, rather than one, for the ranchers and farmers. The first pair ends with S21: *The idea of building a canal turned into an issue,* because this proposition is a consequent of the conjunction of the subtrees, and hence dominates not one but both in the graph. Thereafter, the propositions on the ranchers and farmers run parallel again until a second consequent, namely S25, occurs, which also depends on the conjunction of the parallels.

Now consider the representation of the most interesting aspects of the text, namely the macrolevel constituents, their parallels, and also the major distinctions. The main ideas of the proposed representation appear in Figs. 8.3 and 8.4. The method by which these have been derived as a substantial simplification of the detailed representation (not shown) is as follows. First, the highest levels are graphed conventionally, that is, each node and arc individually. But each lower level subtree is collapsed to a single node, thus disregarding the internal structure of that subtree. This yields Figure 8.3. Next, the procedure is iterated, once for each of the previously collapsed subtrees. Each is expanded top-down. Again, the expansion stops at some level, below which the remaining subtrees are collapsed. This yields Figure 8.4. Here the arbitrarily chosen termination of the expansion is the highest level at which the subtree for the decision on the majority will is separated from the subtree on the execution of that will. The iteration could have been continued several more times, but the graph rapidly becomes complex, owing especially to the subtle distinctions discussed earlier. For the purpose here these Figs. 8.3 and 8.4 will suffice, although large subtrees remain collapsed (especially in IAR).

Let us consider Figure 8.3. It is a top-down expansion to the point that shows, for this one text, the main story grammar constituents and their interconnections. The figure is to be read as follows: of the major constituents defined previously, each one enclosed in square brackets has been collapsed to a

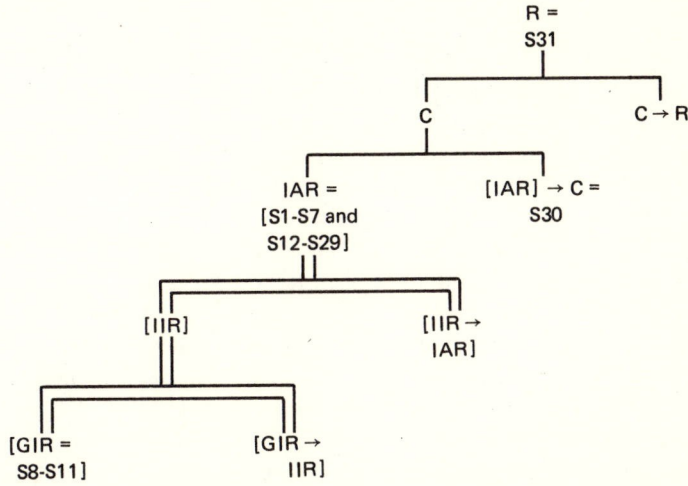

Figure 8.3 *Circle Island* text structure, much simplified by collapsing entire subtrees into single nodes. Notation: Square brackets denote a subtree whose internal structure (shown in Figure 8.4) has been collapsed; double lines denote subtrees whose internal structures are parallel to one another. Abbreviations: GIR = Generalized Ideal Resolution, IIR = Instantiated Ideal Resolution, IAR = Instantiated Actual Resolution, C = Conflict, R = Resolution.

single node, thus postponing its internal representation to Figure 8.4. Also, a single line arc represents an ordinary nonparallel relation between nodes; a double line arc represents a parallel between subtrees. For example, the fact that GIR is parallel to GIR → IIR, and hence to IIR, is shown for the subtrees as units. Having collapsed the subtrees, the parallels between corresponding individual propositions are not shown. In Figure 8.3 each horizontal arc joins a left-hand, unconditional node to a right-hand, conditional node. The former asserts an antecedent (e.g., [IAR]) while the latter asserts a consequent conditional on that antecedent (e.g., [IAR] → C). Thus, the consequence relationship is denoted by an arrow, continuing to suppress the distinction among kinds of consequence. The relation, shown by a horizontal arc, between an unconditional node and its conditional counterpart is conjunction (&)—for example, the conjunction of [IAR] and [IAR] → C. Then, the consequent of the conjunction, C in this example, is graphed directly above the conjunction. Clearly, the graph is a direct representation of the main constituents and their interconnections as proposed in the preceding section.

The three panels of Figure 8.4 show the expansion of the three unconditional subtrees, GIR, IIR, and IAR, respectively. From these three the expansion of the corresponding conditional subtrees is immediate. The expansions are developed as follows: each of the three subtree names now becomes the superordinate of its own subtree in a panel of the figure. In other words, GIR, IIR, and IAR is each derived from its own antecedents. Because many of the parallel propositions have to be inferred, the symbol $\emptyset$ is introduced to denote each such inference. The graph strikes a balance between explicitness and compactness, for the corresponding sentences have been inserted at most left-hand nodes but not at right-hand nodes. Not surprisingly, a few inference rules besides the single rule *modus ponens: X & $(X → Y) → Y$* of the preceding figure are now needed. Particularly, these are *transitivity: $(X → Y$ & $Y → Z) → (X → Z)$* and *modus ponens* with a relational argument: X & $(X → (Y → Z)) → (Y → Z)$. Now the representation begins to bring out the lower levels of the structure. Reading downward, each of the three main resolutions is now subdivided into its own C and $C → R$ antecedents. At this lower level the instantiated conflict is the canal issue. Also, now some of the internal correspondences within the main parallels can be seen, by locating corresponding nodes across the three panels of Figure 8.4. Beyond parallelism, the further elaboration of IAR alone is shown in the lower right-hand sector of Figure 8.4(c).

Other graphing principles have also been implemented in Figure 8.4 though a few (e.g., the S4-S5, S4-S16 divergence) await still further expansion of the graph. Note that S12-S13 on the habitual features of the government is grouped with its consequents rather than with its presuppositions, in IAR rather than in GIR. Also, S1-S7, including, for example, S5: *The ranches are less affected by the lack of fresh water,* is properly shown twice as an antecedent. This can be inferred to have been a contributing cause both for the emergence of

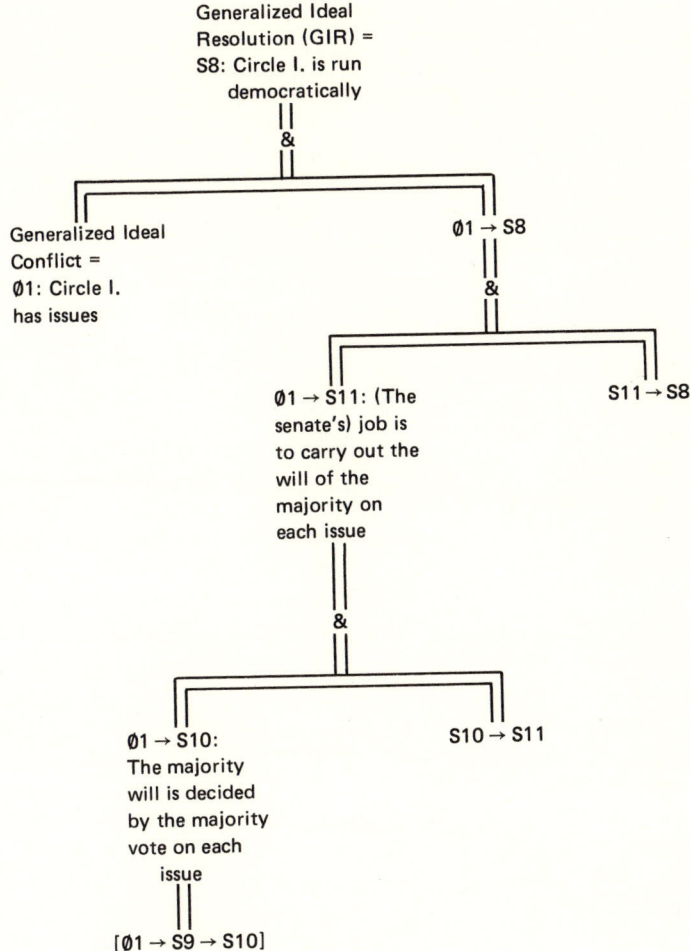

Figure 8.4 (a) Internal structure of the GIR unconditional subtree of Figure 8.3. Notation: Øi denotes an implicit proposition, numbered sequentially; *s* denotes subjunctive sentence mood phraseable as *It was supposed to be the case.* . . .

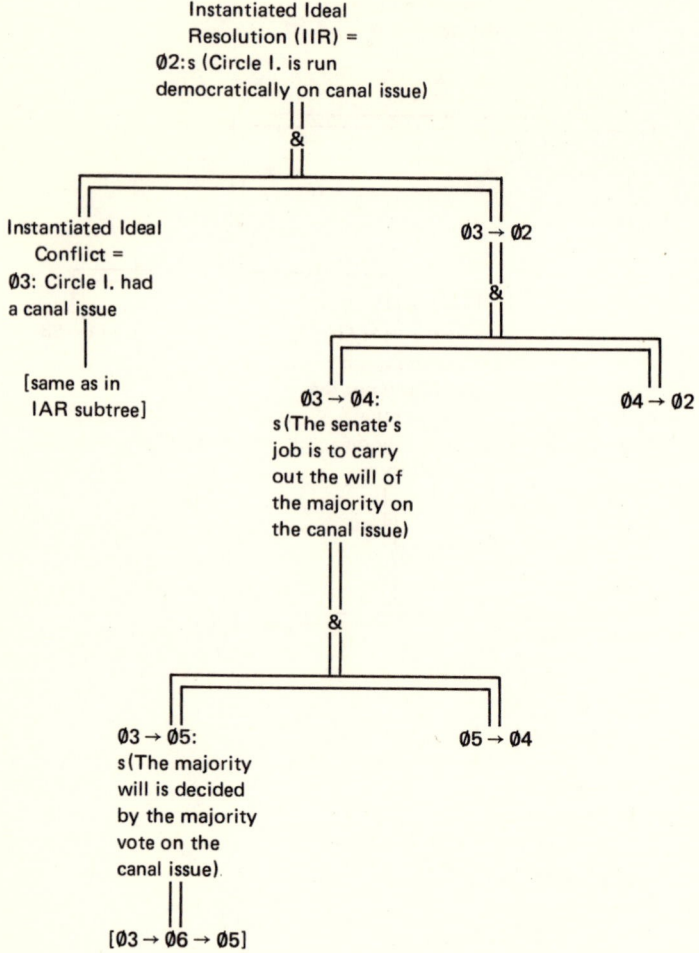

Figure 8.4 (b) Internal structure of the IIR unconditioned subtree of Figure 8.3.

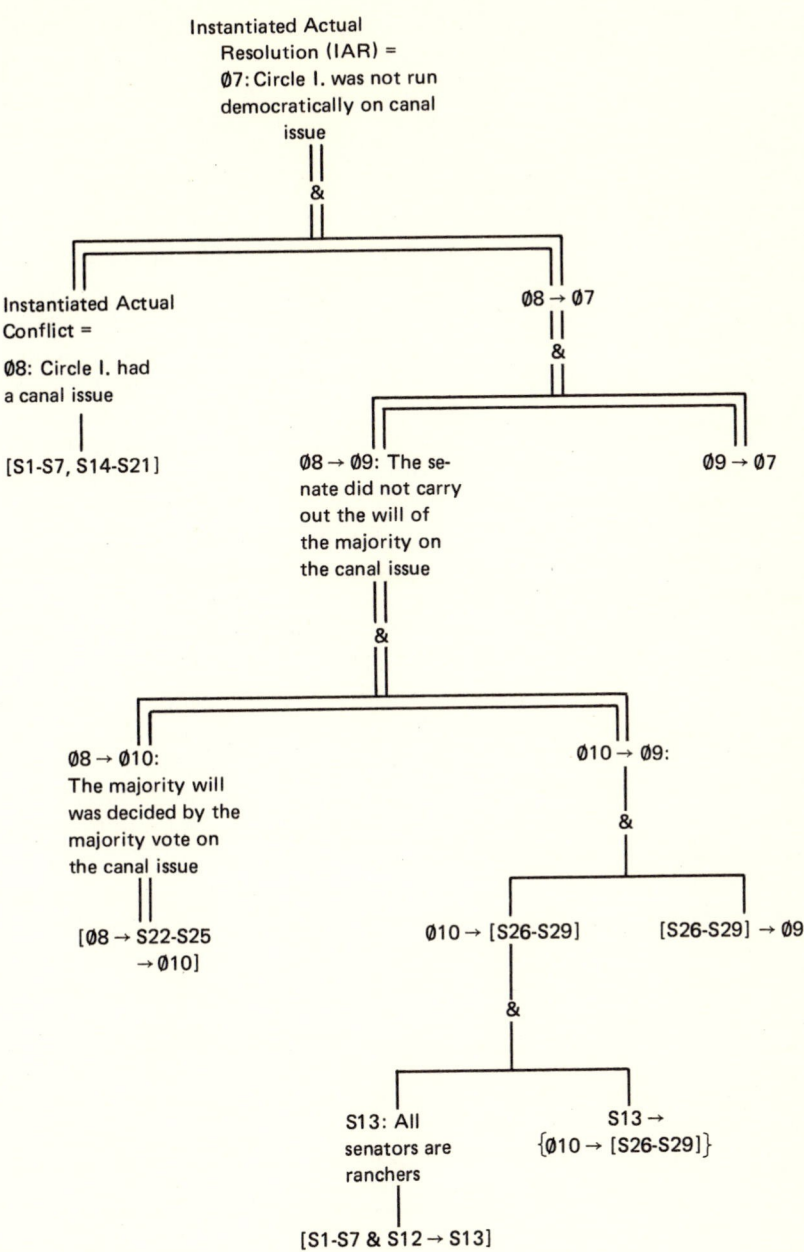

Figure 8.4 (c)   Internal structure of the IAR subtree of Figure 8.3.

the canal issue conflict (∅8: *Circle Island had a canal issue*) and also ultimately for the manner in which the conflict at this level was resolved (via a chain one key node of which is S13: *All senators are ranchers*). We can also observe that by taking Figures 8.3 and 8.4 together one traces out the paths that in Figure 8.2 were abbreviated by ellipses.

Perhaps the most complex aspect of *Circle Island* is its pattern of fairly subtle distinctions. The present remarks are intended only to establish that what must somehow be represented in an intricate interlocking of propositions and not a simple pattern of connections. Many of the propositions in question are only implicit in the surface text, providing further support for the claim that many inferences contribute to tying the text together. The nature of the complexity can be abstractly described as the simultaneous development of multiple interrelated distinctions. That is, major subtrees of the text involve not just a single distinction (viz., *A canal* vs. *a canal that will carry water* vs. *a canal that is large*) or even a "two dimensional" distinction (viz., this distinction crossed with the distinction among the verbs *will (want), vote,* and *build*) but at least a three-dimensional distinction (viz, this distinction crossed again with *farmers, ranchers, majority, minority,* and *senators* as agents). Ignoring any additional sources of complexity, the general idea of this "design" is shown in Table 8.1. Of course, this table pertains only to those parts of the text that develop the distinction in question; the beginning and the ending are less complex. Altogether there are (3 verbs × 3 objects × 5 agents =) 45 propositions classified in Table 8.1. Each has one of three possible truth values: true, false, or unspecified. Admittedly, not all of the 45 combinations occur in the text. For example, the senators *qua* senators are the only agents of *build*, though they are not agents of *vote*. If anything, incompleteness in a "design" of this sort is a further complication rather than a simplification.

Nevertheless, the crux of the complexity lies not in the classification itself but in the interrelations, stated or implied, among classified propositions. What the unfolding of this particular skeletal structure actually amounts to is a succession of derivations, either affirmations or negations, of table entries as

Table 8.1 Some of the Orthogonal Distinctions Stated or Implied in *Circle Island*[a]

Verb	Object		
	Canal	Canal that would carry water	Canal that is large
Will (want)	f./r.,m./m'.,s.	f./r.,m./m'.,s.	f./r.,m./m'.,s.
Vote	f./r.,m./m'.,s.	f./r.,m./m'.,s.	f./r.,m./m'.,s.
Build	f./r.,m./m'.,s.	f./r.,m./m'.,s.	f./r.,m./m'.,s.

[a]Abbreviations for the agents: f./r. = farmers-ranchers contrast, m./m'. = majority-minority contrast, s. = senators.

consequents of other derivations already derived. The particular derivational sequence exhibited in the text is a significant source of complexity. Instead of proceeding in some simple sequence, such as one attribute at a time, there are frequent shifts: from the farmers' and ranchers' wants, to their votes, to the majority vote, to the majority will, to the senate's will, and so on. Compounded with this is concomitant variation in the object, the canal attribute[13]. Indeed, toward the end these object implications (particularly, that from *The senate did not build a large canal* to *The senate did not build a canal that would carry water*) finally emerge and trigger the government crisis. It might be added that another form of complexity, not shown in Table 8.1, is the asymmetric development of nontabled antecedents of the tabled propositions. For example, such antecedents involving ecology are explicit with *ranchers* as the agent of *want*, but any parallel with *farmers* is problematic.

8.4 CONCLUSIONS

We will now venture a few final thoughts on both the theory itself and on possible applications in psycholinguistic research. A basic tenet of our approach has been that detailed descriptive analysis of texts is a necessary accompaniment, and to some extent a predecessor, of more abstract formulations such as text grammars. A descriptive approach, however, can by now be seen as relying on principles of its own. Remarkably complex text structures, especially from the standpoint of inference, were revealed for at least the last two or three of the five passages analyzed. This discovery provided the occasion for observing that complex passages are the very ones that most strongly demand a theory to guide the analysis. At the same time, these complex passages are the ones that most dramatically expose a theory's flaws. Even in the best of linguistic worlds— namely a text that is unambiguous both structurally and semantically—there may be complexities that resist a cursory analysis; complex organization is by no means necessarily equatable with disorganization. We should not have expected otherwise. After all, text complexity stems from the great expressive power of natural language. A myriad of meanings can be communicated, in a range of linguistic forms and styles suited to the pragmatic context.

If, as claimed, description is a necessary precursor to more abstract theorizing, we should expect abstractions derived from a descriptive theory to differ nontrivially from ones derived in other ways. This expectation is upheld, if one can generalize from the story grammar representations of *Circle Island*. The representation developed here is appreciably different from the ones previously

---

[13]Even this statement is an oversimplification, in that the formal analysis requires many nested relations, such as *(farmers vote . . . → farmers want . . .) → (majority vote . . . → majority will . . .)*.

proposed without benefit of a deep inferential analysis. Furthermore, the text categories suggested by the descriptive analysis are also candidates for inclusion in text grammars more general than story grammars.

Prior to this Chapter 8 story grammar representation, the descriptive method led in Chapters 2-7 to the development and subsequent application of some principles of text inference. The inference principles themselves amounted to a text level development of the linguistic-logical notions of consequent and presupposition. This development emphasized the role of such inferences in contributing to a text's cohesion. Advantages and limitations of the inference principles were noted. One very significant limitation is that the theory lacks a world knowledge component, a mental "encyclopedia," which could be invoked to generate inferences as candidates for inclusion in the representation. An advantage of the inference principles is that they enable a more rigorous derivation of a text's structure. Nonrigorous descriptions tend to be less precise and overly influenced by the subjective salience of a particular inference or global schema. Identification of inferences is also necessary for studies on what types of text information are frequently left implicit and why; knowing what could have been present is necessary in order to detect its absence. Another application, at least for texts such as *History,* is to the search for hidden assumptions in an argument.

Apart from text inference in particular, some support for a descriptive approach can be found in the finding that the structures of the brief texts analyzed turned out to differ markedly from one another in some significant respect. Premature induction of an abstract theory might forfeit the opportunity to appreciate this diversity. Exactly where to strike the balance between description and abstraction of a text grammar is a difficult question, probably one that is largely a matter of judgment. The number of descriptions developed here, namely five, is hardly a broad inductive base. On the other hand, in relation to available formulations the theory is an advance. Progress is cumulative: The intent has been to develop a framework within which future theoretical insights can be accommodated as they occur, without either drastic modification or elaboration of the principles.

Another tenet has been that text description is multisided. Though the emphasis has been on inference, attention has also been given to the description of old/new information, lexical relations, text categories, text abstracts, and so on. In each of Chapters 4-7 a detailed description ended with a summary of roughly a dozen different facets of that passage. Of course, an even richer description would have been possible had other levels of analysis been included. For example, the inclusion of the perspective of literary criticism would show that in *State* Thoreau is writing as an acerbic critic. One might even include a description of the pragmatic context, notably the sociopolitical circumstances under which *Civil Disobedience* was composed. Stylistic factors, too, have been only superficially treated in this volume. The allusive style of *Operation,* for example, appears less incongruous if one thinks of allusion as being akin to euphemism and circumlocution, devices resorted to when discussing unpleasant topics. Still, within the self-imposed text level boundary of the theory, the descriptions in Chapters 4-7 appear reasonably complete.

Though the question of psycholinguistic significance of the theory has been touched upon only in general terms, a number of observations can be suggested. Some are methodological, involving the selection or construction of passages for experiments on comprehension and memory. For instance, the demonstrable diversity of text structures argues for caution in generalizing experimental findings from a small sample of texts to a wider population. From this standpoint it would be desirable to sample a wide range of text structures. Unfortunately, this is often not feasible in practice, because the research hypothesis may require texts that are identical except for the structural variables being investigated. Descriptive analysis brings into sharper focus the structural differences between texts, thus calling even more attention to text variables that ideally would be controlled in experiments. This conclusion reinforces the argument for constructing text materials as some researchers have done, namely by preparing versions that are identical except for the variables being studied.

Another valid methodological precept, mentioned in Chapter 1, comes from applying the familiar competence-performance distinction to text research. A researcher is handicapped in formulating and testing performance hypotheses unless an adequate conceptualization of the structure, the competence component, is available. A striking example, of course, is text inference. Unless the potential inferences have been systematically identified beforehand, one cannot seriously investigate the performance question of exactly which inferences a reader will draw as a function of individual and task variables. In addition to inferential selectivity, there is also the matter of inferential depth. For example, once the inference potential of *Circle Island* has been realized, its utility for research on the role of inferences in comprehension is more keenly appreciated. Do text revisions that highlight the parallels enhance comprehension? What might the cognitive effect of emphasizing the generalization-instantiation or idealization-actualization relations be? Does a presupposition organization facilitate comprehension more effectively than a premise organization? Or more specifically, does the linear distance between some antecedents and their consequents in a topical organization occasion the forgetting of such antecedents, thereby reducing the subjective cohesion? Psycholinguistic questions such as these can profitably be posed and investigated within the framework developed here.

References

Anderson, J. R. *Language, memory, and thought.* Hillsdale, NJ: Lawrence Erlbaum Associates, 1976.

Bransford, J., Barclay, J., & Franks, J. Sentence memory: A constructive vs. interpretive approach. *Cognitive Psychology,* 1972, 3, 193-209.

Brockway, J., Chmielewski, D., & Cofer, C. N. Remembering prose: Productivity and accuracy constraints in recognition memory. *Journal of Verbal Learning and Verbal Behavior,* 1974, 13, 194-208.

Carroll, J. B., & Freedle, R. O. *Language comprehension and the acquisition of knowledge.* Washington, DC: Winston, 1972.

Chafe, W. L. *Meaning and the structure of language.* Chicago: University of Chicago Press, 1970.

Chafe, W. L., Discourse structure and human knowledge. In J. B. Carroll & R. O. Freedle (Eds.), *Language comprehension and the acquisition of knowledge.* Washington, DC: Winston, 1972.

Chase, J. H. *No orchids for Miss Blandish.* New York: Avon, 1961.

Crothers, E. J. *Paragraph structure description:* Vols. I and II. (Tech. Rep. No. 40). Boulder, CO: University of Colorado, Institute for the Study of Intellectual Behavior, May 1975.

Crothers, E. J. Memory structure and the recall of discourse. In J. B. Carroll & R. O. Freedle (Eds.), *Language comprehension and the acquisition of knowledge.* Washington, DC: Winston, 1972.

Crothers, E. J. Inference and coherence. *Discourse Processes,* 1978, 1, 51-71. (a)

Crothers, E. J. Text linguistics issues from a text representation perspective. In J. S. Petöfi (Ed.), *Text vs. sentence.* Hamburg: Buske Verlag, 1978. (b)

Dawes, R. M. Memory and distortion of meaningful verbal material. *British Journal of Psychology,* 1966, 57, 77-86.

deVilliers, P. Imagery and theme in recall of connected discourse. *Journal of Experimental Psychology,* 1974, 103, 263-268.

van Dijk, T. A. *Some aspects of text grammars.* The Hague: Mouton, 1972.

van Dijk, T. A. Text grammar and text logic. In J. S. Petöfi & H. Rieser (Eds.), *Studies in text grammar*. Dordrecht: Reidel, 1973.

van Dijk, T. A. Connectives in grammar and logic. In T. A. van Dijk & J. S. Petöfi (Eds.), *Grammars and descriptions*. Berlin: De Gruyter Press, 1976.

Dooling, D. J., & Lachman, R. Effects of comprehension on retention of prose. *Journal of Experimental Psychology*, 1971, 88, 216-222.

Egner, E. & Devonn, L. E. (Eds.), *The basic writings of Bertrand Russell*. New York: Simon and Schuster, 1967.

Frase, L. Paragraph organization of written materials: The influence of conceptual clusterings upon level of organization. *Journal of Education Psychology*, 1969, 60, 394-401.

Frederiksen, C. H. Acquisition of semantic information from discourse: Effects of repeated exposures. *Journal of Verbal Learning and Verbal Behavior*, 1975, 14, 158-169. (a)

Frederiksen, C. H. Representing logical and semantic structure of knowledge acquired from discourse. *Cognitive Psychology* 1975, 7, 371-458. (b)

Gopnik, M. *Linguistic structures in scientific texts*. The Hague: Mouton, 1972.

Grice, H. P. Logic and conversation. In P. Cole & J. Morgan (Eds.), *Syntax and semantics* (Vol. 3). New York: Academic Press, 1975.

Grimes, J. E. *The thread of discourse*. The Hague: Mouton, 1975.

Halliday, M. A. K. Notes on transitivity and theme in English: II. *Journal of Linguistics*, 1967, 3, 199-244.

Halliday, M. A. K., & Hasan, R. *Cohesion in English*. London: Longmans, 1976.

Harris, Z. S. Discourse analysis: A sample text. *Language*, 1952, 28, 474-494.

Haviland, S. E., & Clark, H. H. What's new? Acquiring new information as a process in comprehension. *Journal of Verbal Learning and Verbal Behavior*, 1974, 13, 512-521.

James, W. *The principles of psychology*. New York: Holt, 1891.

Johnson, R. Recall of prose as a function of the structural importance of the linguistic units. *Journal of Verbal Learning and Verbal Behavior*, 1970, 9, 12-20.

Katz, J. J. *Semantic theory*. New York: Harper & Row, 1972.

Keenan, J. M., & Kintsch, W. The identification of explicitly and implicitly presented information. In W. Kintsch, *The representation of meaning in memory*. Hillsdale, NJ: Lawrence Erlbaum Associates, 1974.

Kieras, D. Problems of reference in text comprehension. Twelfth Annual Carnegie Symposium on Cognition, Pittsburgh: Carnegie-Mellon University, May 1976.

Kintsch, W. *The representation of meaning in memory*. Hillsdale, NJ: Lawrence Erlbaum Associates, 1974.

Kintsch, W. Comprehension and memory of text. In W. K. Estes (Ed.), *Handbook of learning and cognitive processes* (Vol. 5). Hillsdlae, NJ: Lawrence Erlbaum Associates, 1976.

Kintsch, W., & van Dijk, T. A. Comments on se repelle et on résume des histories. *Languages*, 1975, 40, 98-116.

Kintsch, W., & Keenan, J. M. Recall of propositions as a function of their position in the hierarchical structure. In W. Kintsch, *The representation of meaning in memory*. Hillsdale, NJ: Lawrence Erlbaum Associates, 1974.

Kintsch, W., Kozminsky, E., Streby, W., McKoon, G. A., & Keenan, J. M. Comprehension and recall of text as a function of content variables. *Journal of Verbal Learning and Verbal Behavior*, 1975, 14, 196-214.

Koen, F., Becker, A., & Young, R. The psychological reality of the paragraph. *Journal of Verbal Learning and Verbal Behavior*, 1969, 8, 49-53.

Longacre, R. E. *Hierarchy and universality of discourse constituents in New Guinea languages: texts*. Washington, DC: Georgetown University Press, 1972.

Loriot, J., & Hollenbach, B. Shipibo paragraph structure. *Foundation of Language*, 1970, 6, 43-66.

Mandler, J. M., & Johnson, N. S. Remembrance of things parsed: story structure and recall. *Cognitive Psychology*, 1977, **9**, 111-151.

Meyer, B. *The organization of prose and its effects on memory*. Amsterdam: North Holland, 1975.

Meyer, B. & McConkie, G. What is recalled after hearing a passage? *Journal of Educational Psychology*, 1973, **65**, 109-117.

Paris, S. G., & Upton, L. R. Children's memory for inferential relationships in prose. *Child Development*, 1976, **47**, 660-668.

Perfetti, C. A., & Goldman, S. R. Thematization and sentence retrieval. *Journal of Verbal Learning and Verbal Behavior*, 1974, **13**, 70-79.

Petöfi, J. S. Towards and empirically motivated grammatical theory of verbal texts. In J. S. Petöfi & H. Rieser (Eds.), *Studies in text grammar*. Dordrecht: Reidel, 1973.

Pike, K. L. Language in relation to a unified theory of the structure of human behavior, Part 1. Glendale, CA: Summer Institute of Linguistics, 1954. Second Ed. The Hague: Mouton, 1967.

Pompi, K., & Lachman, R. Surrogate processes in the short-term retention of connected discourse. *Journal of Experimental Psychology*, 1967, **75**, 143-150.

Quillian, M. R. The teachable language comprehender: A simulation program and theory of language. *Communications of the Association for Computing Machinery*, 1969, **12**, 459-476.

Rieger, C. J. Conceptual memory and inference. In R. C. Schank, *Conceptual information processing*. Amsterdam: North Holland, 1975.

Rosenberg, S. Associative facilitation in the recall and recognition of nouns embedded in connected discourse. *Journal of Experimental Psychology*, 1968, 78, 254-260.

Ross, J. R. Ross-McCawley discussion. In W. B. Weimer & D. S. Palermo (Eds.), *Cognition and the symbolic processes*. Hillsdale, NJ: Lawrence Erlbaum Associates, 1974.

Rumelhart, D. E., Notes on a schema for stories. In D. Bobrow & A. Collins (Eds.), *Representation and understanding: Studies in cognitive science*. New York: Academic Press, 1975.

Rumelhart, D. E., Lindsay, P. H., & Norman, D. A. A process model for long-term memory. In E. Tulving & W. Donaldson (Eds.), *Organization of memory*. New York: Academic Press, 1972.

Sanders, G. A. On the natural domain of grammar. *Linguistics*, 1970, **63**, 51-123.

Schank, R. *Conceptual information processing*. Amsterdam: North Holland, 1975. (a)

Schank, R. The structure of episodes in memory. In D. Bobrow & A. Collins (Eds.), *Representation and understanding: Studies in cognitive science*. New York: Academic Press, 1975. (b)

Simmons, R. F., & Slocum, J. Generating English discourse from semantic networks. *Communications of the Association for Computing Machinery*, 1972, **15**, 891-905.

Thoreau, H. D. Resistance to civil government. In E. P. Peabody (Ed.), *Aesthetic papers*. Boston, 1849. Reprinted in London: Peace Pledge Union, 1943.

Thorndyke, P. W. The role of inferences in discourse comprehension. *Journal of Verbal Learning and Verbal Behavior*, 1976, **15**, 437-446.

Thorndyke, P. W. Cognitive structures in comprehension and memory of narrative discourse. *Cognitive Psychology*, 1977, **9**, 77-110.

Winograd, T. Understanding natural language. *Cognitive Psychology*, 1972, **3**, 1-191.

Yuille, J. C., & Paivio, A. Abstractness and recall of connected discourse. *Journal of Experimental Psychology*, 1969, **82**, 467-471.

Author Index

Numbers in *italics* refer to pages on which the complete references are listed.

Kintsch, W., 12, 15, 94, *116*
Koen, F., 12, *116*
Kozminsky, E., 12, *116*

Lachman, R., 3, 12, 15, *116, 117*
Lindsay, P.H., 6, *117*
Longacre, R.E., 11, *116*
Loriot, J., 11, *116*

Mandler, J.M., 94, *117*
McConkie, G., 12, *117*
McKoon, G.A., 12, *116*
Meyer, B., 11, 12, *117*

Norman, D.A., 6, *117*

Paivio, A., 3, 12, *117*
Paris, S.G., 12, *117*
Perfetti, C.A., 12, *117*
Petofi, J.S., 5, *117*
Pompi, K., 3, 12, 15, *117*

Quillian, M.R., 6, *117*

Rieger, C.J., 13, *117*
Rosenberg, S., 12, *117*
Ross, J.R., 6, *117*
Rumelhart, D.E., 6, 8, 13, 94, *117*

Sanders, G.A., 12, *117*
Schank, R., 6, 7, 8, 13, *117*
Simmons, R.F., 13, *117*
Slocum, J., 13, *117*
Streby, W., 12, *116*

Thoreau, H.D., 3, 45, *117*
Thorndyke, P.W., 12, 92, 94, *117*

Upton, L.R., 12, *117*

Winograd, T., 8, 9, 13, *117*

Young, R., 12, *116*
Yuille, J.C., 3, 12, *117*

Subject Index

Conversational postulates, 19

Criteria for inferences, 7-8, 9, 20-21, 26

Cross-hierarchic connection, 58, 62, 64-66, 69, 88, 97, 103

D

Definite noun phrase, 7, 12, 22-26, 66-69, 78-80, 89-90, 91

Definitions, 16-31

Derivation of text structure, 2, 6, 9, 12, 52-56, 63-68, 77-80, 86-90, 111-112

Descriptive theory, 5, 13, 111

Detailed nature of descriptions, 2, 93

Disjunctive syllogism, 66

Distinctions, 102, 110

Diversity of texts, 3-4, 17, 35, 41, 43-44, 112, 113 (*See also* Comparison of texts)

E

Editing, text, 5, 26

Element of proposition, 22-26, 28, 53, 67-69, 78-80, 89-90, 91, 95

Endophoric and exophoric references, 18

Enthymeme, 11

Evaluation of theory, 9, 11, 93, 111-114

Excerpts, 15

Explicit text, 26-31, 53-56, 68, 80, 90

Extensions of theory, 92-114

F

Figurative interpretation, 31, 56

Frequency tabulations, 16-31

G

Generality of theory, 94

Global inference, 58, 63-64, 69, 93-94

Grammar, text, 5, 12, 94, 111-112

H

Hierarchy, text, 12, 13, 39, 42-43, 46, 52-53, 58-63, 69, 70-75, 78, 80, 82-85, 90, 91, 93-94, 97, 99, 102-110

History passage, 15-31, 35-44, 56, 70-81

I

Identity connective, 37-39

Implication, 17 (*See also* Inference of propositions)

Inference, 7, 13, 93-94, 112, 113
   a priori and *a posteriori*, 18-19
   criteria for, 7-8, 9, 20-21, 26
   global, 58, 63-64, 69, 89, 93-94
   logical or semantic, 8, 12, 20, 35-38, 93, 112
   of connectives, 7, 16, 35-41, 49, 53-54, 57, 58-63, 69, 81, 86, 91, 95-96, 98-100, 110
   of elements (reference), 7, 21-26, 53, 67-69, 89-90, 95
   of propositions (implication), 7, 12, 16-21, 64-67, 69, 77-78, 81, 86-89, 91, 95-96, 101, 110

Informal phrasing of underlying structure, 50, 62, 75, 82-83

Information: old, new and contrastive, 12, 32-35, 56, 69, 81, 91, 112

Intracategory relations, 7, 12, 28-30, 33, 51, 55-56, 68, 69, 80-81, 91, 112

Issues, 4-10

J

Judgements in inferencing, 8, 20, 30-31

L

Level of analysis, 6, 13, 112-113

Lexical relations, 7, 12, 28-30, 33, 51, 55-56, 68, 69, 80, 81, 91, 112